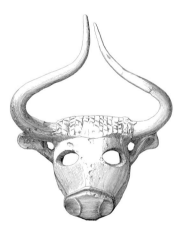

The Barbar Temples

Appendices

The Carlsberg Foundation's Gulf Project

The Barbar Temples

Volume 2. Appendices

With contributions by
H. Hellmuth Andersen, Pernille Bangsgaard,
Dennis L. Heskel, Flemming Højlund,
Edward Sangmeister and Margareta Tengberg

Jutland Archaeological Society

Moesgaard Museum
Ministry of Information, Bahrain

The Barbar Temples

H.Hellmuth Andersen & Flemming Højlund © 2003

ISBN 87-88415-27-9
ISSN 0107-2854

Jutland Archaeological Society Publications vol. 48

Editor: Flemming Højlund
English translation and revision: Geoffrey Bibby and Peter Crabb
Layout & cover: Orla Svendsen
Drawings: Orla Svendsen, Jens Kirkeby, Louise Hilmar, Flemming Bau,
Elsebet Morville
Photographs: P.V. Glob, H. Hellmuth Andersen, Lennart Larsen,
Peder Mortensen, P. Dehlholm, Rogvi Johansen, G. Franceschi
Printed by Narayana Press
Type: Palatino
Paper: Arctic Silk 130 g

Published by:
Jutland Archaeological Society
Moesgaard
DK-8270 Højbjerg

in association with
the Moesgaard Museum and
the Ministry of Information, Bahrain

Distributed by
Aarhus University Press
Langelandsgade 177
DK-8200 Aarhus N
www.unipress.dk

Published with the financial support of the Carlsberg Foundation

Contents

Appendix 1. Animal Bones from the Barbar Temple

By Pernille Bangsgaard

Introduction

The faunal remains presented here were recovered from the temples at Barbar during the Danish archaeological expeditions in 1954 to 1961. The material dates from the centuries around 2000 BC, see vol. 1, fig. 266. The animal bones found in a re-used well at the site, dating to the 9th century AD, have been published elsewhere (Bangsgaard 2001).

The faunal material from the Barbar temples includes 2415 fragments, of which 1232 remain unidentified and 1183 have been assigned to family or to species (see table 1). The identified material contains at least 9 species, which include both domesticated and wild mammals, a bird bone and also a significant amount of fish bones. The material varies in preservation, but is generally fragmentary and fragile, revealing significant post-depositional damage. The faunal material comes mainly from Temples I and II, with a small group of material with an insecure dating. There were no bones from a secure Temple III context.

The analysis was carried out at the Zoological Museum, Copenhagen University, using the extensive comparative collection there, but some of the fish bones and the bird bone were analysed at the Ludwig-Maximilian University in Munich, Institute of Palaeoanatomy.[1]

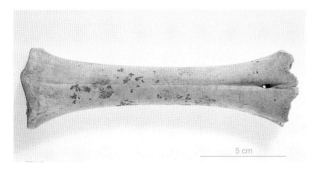

Fig. 1: A juvenile metacarpal of cattle, *Bos taurus*.

Domesticated Mammals

By far the largest group within the faunal material from Barbar is that of the domesticated animals, constituting over 86% of the identified material:

	Number	Weight (in g)
Cattle, *Bos taurus*	328	5537
Large ruminant	444	783
Sheep, *Ovis aries*	50	352
Goat, *Capra hircus*	20	106
Sheep/Goat, *Ovis/Capra*	178	664

Cattle, Bos taurus

328 fragments have been identified as cattle, making cattle the best-represented species at Barbar, both in terms of the total number and the weight of the bones. Due to the fragmentary state of these and a lack of the larger limb-bones from this species, the MNI number (Minimal Number of Individuals) is only 23. Considering the high number of fragments, the MNI number is presumably much lower than it would have been if a more complete ensemble of the cattle bones had been preserved.

Another large group of domesticated animals comprises the large ruminants. This group mostly consists of very fragmented and for some part severely burnt fragments of teeth. It has therefore been impossible to come to a final identification to species level. But as cattle are the only identified large ruminants from the site, the probability is that this group also comprises cattle. This large ruminant group is therefore placed with the cattle group.

[1] I would like to express my gratitude to Knud Rosenlund, Zoological Museum in Copenhagen, for his kind help through the entire process and to Angela von den Driesch, Ludwig-Maximilian University, for her unstinting help with the identification of fish and bird bones. I am also indebted to the following for advice and suggestions to improve the manuscript: Flemming Højlund, Hans-Peter and Margarethe Uerpmann and David Warburton.

7

	Cattle *Bos taurus*	Large ruminants	Sheep *Ovis aries*	Goat *Capra hircus*	Goat/sheep *Capra hircus/ Ovis aries*	Gazelle *Gazella sp.*	Desert hare *Lepus capensis*	Socotra Cormorant *Phalacrocorax nigrogularis*	Fish	Unidentified
Cranium	25	12	-	1	1	-	-	-	41*	3
Mandible	17	66	-	-	1	-	1	-	-	8
Loose teeth	210	357	-	-	35	-	-	-	-	39
Vertebrae	5	4	-	-	12	-	-	-	71	1
Ribs	24	5	-	-	19	-	-	-	-	16
Scapula	5	-	2	-	2	-	-	-	-	-
Humerus	3	-	2	1	3	-	-	-	-	-
Radius	3	-	1	-	7	-	-	1	-	1
Ulna	2	-	-	-	1	-	-	-	-	-
Pelvis	1	-	-	2	-	-	-	-	-	-
Femur	2	-	1	-	5	-	-	-	-	-
Tibia	2	-	-	-	4	-	-	-	-	-
Patella	-	-	1	-	-	-	-	-	-	-
Carpal/tarsal	8	-	4	2	3	-	-	-	-	-
Metacarpal/tarsal	10	-	16	7	76	2	-	-	-	-
Phalanges	11	-	23	7	9	-	-	-	-	-
Unidentified	-		-	-	-	-	-	-	47	1164
Total	328	444	50	20	178	2	1	1	159	1232
Total weight (in g.)	5537	783	352	106	664	26	1	1	967	2024
MNI	23	-	10	3	19	1	1	1	-	-

Table 1: The distribution of the animal bones from the Barbar Temple

*In this category two complete crania have been added, counted each as a single fragment.

Considering the amount of usable meat per animal, it becomes obvious that cattle were the dominant species at Barbar. Cattle are by far the largest contributor of meat: combined with the large ruminants they account for 32% of the total number of bones and 65% of the identified bones. As for the weight, the numbers are even more convincing, since cattle account for 60% of the total weight and 75% of the weight of the identified bones.

It is worth noting the scarcity of larger limb-bones of cattle. This can partly be attributed to the generally poor preservation of the faunal material. The problem of preservation is known to affect the larger limb-bones and also the fragile rib and cranium bones, whereas the small and more compact bones of the foot often have a higher rate of survival, but this is perhaps not the only explanation.

The number of preserved fragments of bones that carry less meat (cranium and ribs) is higher than expected, when compared to the number of long-bones (humerus, femur, radius, and tibia), which have a thicker layer of muscles. This is significant, since the number of ribs and parts of the cranium found in the excavation should have been as severely affected as that of the limb-bones, if poor preservation was the only factor involved.

Age Distribution. Due to the scarcity of larger limb-bones and the fragmentary state of the teeth found at Barbar, the number of fragments suitable for age determination is very small. However, a number of metapodials and phalanges allow for some indication of age distribution for the cattle group (see table 2).

Bone	Unfused	Fused	Number	Time of Fusion
Ulna, proximal	1	-	2	3½ - 4 years
Tibia, distal	-	1	2	2- 2½ years
Metapodium, distal	7	-	10	2 - 2½ years
P. Phalanges, proximal	1	4	6	1½ - 2 years

Table 2: Time of fusion for the cattle bones

Bone	n	1	2	3	4	x
Cornus						
45	1		36.0			36.0
46	1		47.0			47.0
M3 inf.						
10A	2	34.0		38.0		36.0
10B	2	10.5		14.0		12.3
Scapula						
GLP	1		59.5			59.5
LG	1		54.5			54.5
Pelvis						
LAR	1		57.5			57.5
Metacarpal						
Bp	1		60.5			60.5
Proximal Phalanges						
Glpe	1		57.0			57.0
Bp	2	27.5		33.0		30.3
SD	3	23.0	25.5	26.0		24.8
Bd	4	24.5	26.0	27.5	28.5	26.6
Medial Phalanges						
GL	2	37.5		39.0		38.3
Bp	4	27.0	28.5	31.5	32.0	29.8
SD	4	22.0	24.0	24.0	24.5	23.6
Bd	1		24.5			24.5

Table 3: Measurements of the cattle bones (in mm).

For the indication of the youngest possible age of butchering, four fused and one unfused phalanx (fusion taking place around the age of 1½ to 2 years) were examined, indicating that the majority were butchered after this age. Also one unfused ulna (fusion around the age of 3½ to 4 years) was included in the study, and although it is a very small sample, it does indicate that at least the majority of the cattle butchered here were between the ages of 1½ and 4 years. Furthermore, one fused tibia and seven unfused metapodials (fusion around the age of 2-2½ years) were suitable for study. The indication of this distribution, as the number of unfused bones is so much higher than the number of fused bones, is that the age of butchering was probably less than 2½ years. So the evidence suggests that cattle were generally butchered between the age of 1 and 2½ years. The age of fusion is based on Schmid's work (Schmid 1972 p. 75).

Body Size. All bones that were fused and in good condition were measured (see table 3) according to von den Driesch (1976). The number of bones measured is low. Apart from a single scapula and pelvis, they are restricted to bones from the lower part of the limbs, or teeth and horn core.

When comparing the measurements of cattle from Barbar with material from Qala'at al-Bahrain there is a point worth noting. The two groups of faunal material are roughly of the same period and the same area, but there is a minor difference in size. The Barbar measurements are slightly higher than those of the material from Qala'at al-Bahrain. The difference is not great but consistent for all comparable measurements.

Cut-marks. A very small number of cut-marks were found on the cattle bones. The small number is probably to some extent due to the poor state of preservation for the bones, for many have a degraded exterior surface that does not allow for detection of cut-marks. Seven cut-marks were found, and they are mainly located on the bones of the lower leg, such as phalanges and metapodia. They are all consistent with marks left by the process of dismembering.

Sheep and Goat, *Ovis aries* and *Capra hircus*

The only other domesticated animal found at Barbar is the sheep and goat group, which is the second largest group. Whenever possible the bones from the small ungulates were identified to species, but for the majority it was impossible to distinguish between sheep and goat due to the very fragmentary state of the material. Contrary to most sites in the Middle East, the sheep and goat group is not the dominant component at the Barbar temples.

Fig. 2: To the left two proximal phalanges from sheep, *Ovis aries*, and to the right two from goat, *Capra hircus*.

Bone	Unfused	Fused	Number	Time of Fusion
Humerus, distal	-	2	2	¼ year
Radius, distal	1	-	1	3½ years
Femur, distal	1	-	1	3½ years
Metapodium, distal	4	3	16	1⅔ - 2 years
P. Phalanges, proximal	-	16	19	½ - ¾ years

Table 4: Time of fusion for the sheep bones

Bone	Unfused	Fused	Number	Time of Fusion
Humerus, distal	-	1	1	¼ year
Metapodium, distal	1	-	7	1⅔ - 2 years
P. Phalanges, proximal	2	1	3	½ - ¾ years

Table 5: Time of fusion for the goat bones

Bone	Unfused	Fused	Number	Time of Fusion
Vertebrae	9	-	12	4 - 5 years
Humerus, proximal	2*	1	3	3½ years
Radius, proximal	1*	1	7	¼ year
Radius, distal	3*	-	7	3½ years
Femur, proximal	1*	-	5	3 - 3½ years
Femur, distal	1*	-	5	3½ years
Metapodium, distal	20	5	76	1⅔ - 2 years
P. Phalanges, proximal	-	7	9	½ - ⅔ years

* One bone fragment from each of these categories was identified as pullus

Table 6: Time of fusion for the sheep/goat bones

Enough of the sheep and goat bones were identified to species to indicate the actual distribution of the two animals. The bones that could be identified to species indicate that sheep was by far the dominant of the two, for the number of sheep bones is more than twice as high as the number of goat bones.

Age Distribution. The age distribution for sheep and goat calculated from the fusion of the long-bones is generally the same for all three groups (see tables 4-6), and they will therefore be treated as one.

Aside from five bones from very young animals, the evidence suggests that the animals were well above the age of 3 to 9 months old (humerus distal, radius proximal and phalanx proximal). The evidence is compelling for the animals being below the age of 3½ years, since all the vertebrae examined were unfused. Also for the proximal humerus, the distal radius and the femur, 9 out of 10 bones are unfused and thus again indicate that the animals were butchered before the age of 3½ years. For the distal metapodium – where we have the largest col-

Bone	n	1	2	3	4	x
Scapula						
SLG	1	16.5				16.5
GLP	1	28.0				28.0
LP	1	12.0				12.0
Humerus						
Bd	1	26.5				26.5
BT	1	25.5				25.5
Patella						
GB	1	14.5				14.5
Astragalus						
GLl	2	27.5		28.5		28.0
GLm	2	26.0		27.5		26.8
Dl	2	15.5		15.5		15.5
Bd	2	17.5		18.5		18.0
Calcaneus						
GL	2	60.5		61.0		60.8
GB	2	21.5		21.5		21.5
Metacarpal						
GL	2	137.5		154.0		145.8
Bp	8	20.0	21.0	21.5	22.0	22.6
		22.5	23.0	25.0	25.0	
SD	3	12.5	12.5	13.0		12.7
CD	3	34.5	41.0	41.0		38.8
DD	3	9.5	10.0	10.0		9.8
Bd	2	24.0		27.5		25.8
Metatarsal						
Bp	2	18.0		19.0		18.5
SD	1	11.0				11.0
Proximal Phalanges						
Glpe	12	29.5	29.5	31.0	32.0	34.3
		32.0	32.5	33.5	35.5	
		37.0	37.0	40.0	41.5	
Bp	13	10.5	11.0	11.5	11.5	12.3
		11.5	11.5	12.0	12.5	
		12.5	12.5	12.5	13.5	
		15.0				
SD	16	8.0	8.5	8.5	8.5	9.5
		9.0	9.0	9.0	9.5	
		9.5	9.5	9.5	10.5	
		10.5	10.5	10.5	11.5	
Bd	15	9.5	9.5	10.0	10.0	11.3
		10.5	10.5	10.5	11.0	
		11.5	12.0	12.0	12.5	
		12.5	13.0	15.0		
Medial Phalanges						
GL	3	21.0	21.0	25.5		22.5
Bp	3	12.0	12.5	12.5		12.3
SD	3	8.5	9.0	9.5		9.0
Bd	3	9.0	9.5	10.0		9.5

Table 7: Measurements of the sheep bones (in mm)

Bone	n	1	2	3	4	x
Humerus						
Bd	1		31.5			31.5
BT	1		30.5			30.5
Astragalus						
GLl	1		25.5			25.5
GLm	1		23.5			23.5
Dl	1		13.5			13.5
Bd	1		15.5			15.5
Metacarpal						
Bp	1		21.0			21.0
Dp	1		15.0			15.0
Metatarsal						
Bp	4	19.5	19.5	20.5	23.5	20.8
SD	1		11.0			11.0
CD	1		37.5			37.5
Proximal Phalanges						
SD	1		10.0			10.0
Bd	1		11.5			11.5
Medial Phalanges						
GL	1		24.5			24.5
Bp	1		13.5			13.5
SD	1		10.0			10.0
Bd	1		11.0			11.0
Distal Phalanges						
DLS	2		30.5		30.5	30.5

Table 8: Measurements of the goat bones (in mm)

ments were possible. The sheep bones (table 7) are generally smaller than the bones of the same period from Qala'at al-Bahrain. However, the goat bones (table 8) display the same tendencies as cattle, since they are slightly but consistently larger than the equivalent contemporaneous Qala'at al-Bahrain bones (Uerpmann & Uerpmann 1994).

Cut-marks. A small number of cut-marks were found on the sheep and goat bones. As was the case with the cut-marks on cattle, one possible explanation for the low number may well be the poorly preserved surface and generally poor preservation of the faunal material. Only 13 cut-marks were registered, and it was therefore decided to treat sheep and goat bones as one. The cut-marks on the sheep and goat bones are more diverse than the cut-marks on cattle bones, and a wider spectrum of bones is represented. The majority of marks are found on metapodials (6), but they have also been located on vertebrae, humerus, femur, ribs and astragalus. The cut-marks are all consistent with marks made during the process of dismembering.

Wild Mammals

Only three bones were found from wild mammals, two being identified as gazelle and one as desert hare:

	Number	Weight (in g)
Gazelle, *Gazella* sp.	2	26
Desert hare, *Lepus capensis*	1	1

Fig. 3: A metatarsal of gazelle, *Gazella* sp.

Gazelle, *Gazella* sp.

The two bones found were both from adult individuals, but due to the very similar morphology and size of the three gazelle species found in the Gulf area (*Gazella gazella*, *G. dorcas* and *G. subgutturosa*), it was not possible to determine with any certainty which one is represented at Barbar.

Evidence suggests that there may well have been an indigenous population of gazelles on Bahrain, due to the identification of gazelle bones from excavations and based on morphological evidence

lection for comparison – the majority of the bones (25 of 33) are unfused, fusion taking place around the age of 1⅔-2 years, thus all indicating that when butchered, the animals ranged in age from just under a year to just less than three years, with the majority being butchered before the age of 2. This is also supported by the phalanges, where 24 of 26 bones are fused and thus from animals that were butchered after the age of 6-8 months. The lack of older animals is striking, for a population kept for household production necessarily would include a group of older animals for breeding purposes (Payne 1973). The five pullus bones found represent two separate finds, both from Temple II. Four of these bones were found together, probably from a single individual, and are from an animal no more than a few days old. They were found together with a number of fish bones.

Body Size. Measurements were taken for both sheep and goat bones (see tables 7-8). Due to a more diverse collection of bones compared to cattle, a wider spectrum and higher number of measure-

	Spiny-rayed fish Carangidae sp.	Porgies and Breams Sparidae sp.	Toothed Sparus Dentex dentex	Mackerels and Tunnies Scombridea sp.	Narrow-barred Spanish Mackerel Scomberoideus commersonianus	Unidentified fish bones
Premaxilla	-	2	-	-	2	-
Maxilla	-	-	-	-	-	1
Suborbital	-	-	-	-	-	5
Dentary	-	-	-	-	-	11
Angular	-	-	-	-	-	11
Opercle	-	-	-	-	-	1
Cleithrum	-	-	-	-	5	1
Vertebrae	9	15	-	5	-	42
Unidentified	-	-	-	-	-	47
Total	9	17	1*	5	7	102*
Total weight (in g)	85	70	181	18	34	597
MNI	-	-	1	-	3	-

* In each of these categories one complete cranium has been counted as a single fragment.

Table 9: The distribution of the fish bones from the Barbar temples

(Uerpmann & Uerpmann 1994). In recent times, the island of Bahrain has supported a gazelle population that is periodically mixed with animals imported from the Arabian mainland. Some suggest that this mixing is due to a lack of suitable habitat large enough to sustain a healthy gazelle population, exploited for hunting, over a longer period of time (Hill et al. n.d.). This leaves a few possibilities for the bones found at Barbar. It is possible that there already was a population of gazelles on Bahrain at that time. However, animals may have been imported, perhaps from the Arabian Peninsula, either as live animals or as dried meat. But with only two fragments found during excavation, no final conclusion can be made at this point.

Desert hare, Lepus capensis

Only a single fragment has been identified as hare. The bone is a right mandible, without any teeth present. By contrast, hare appears to be more abundant in later periods (see Bangsgaard 2001). The desert hare is still found on the island.

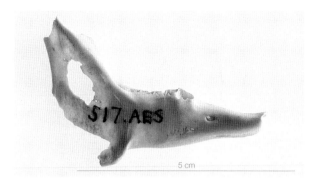

Fig. 4: A mandible of desert hare, *Lepus capensis*.

Birds

Only a single bird bone was found during excavation:

	Number	Weight (in g)
Socotra Cormorant, *Phalacrocorax nigrogularis*	1	1

The find of only one bone from cormorant may be seen as consistent with the fact that today the bird is known only from nearby Hawar Island (Hill et al. n.d.). However, there have been several finds from archaeological sites indicating that the situation was different in the Dilmun period. Finds from Qala'at al-Bahrain indicate that the cormorant was caught in large numbers, although this may merely have been a by-product of fishing with nets (Uerpmann & Uerpmann 1994 and 1997). But as so many cormorant bones are found at the site, it is likely that this bird was eaten regularly, despite the nature of its capture. Later finds from Barbar itself also indicate that this was the case in the Early Islamic period (Bangsgaard 2001).

Fish

The third most numerous group of bones comprised fish:

	Number	Weight (in g)
Spiny-rayed fish, *Carangidae* sp.	9	85
Porgies/ Sea Breams, *Sparidae* sp.	17	70
Toothed Sparus, *Dentex dentex*	1*	181
Mackerels and Tunnies, *Scombridae* sp.	5	18
Narrow-barred Spanish Mackerel, *Scomberoideus commersonianus*	7	34
Unidentified fish	102*	597

* In these categories one complete cranium has been added, counted only as a single fragment. This solution was chosen for all tables recording fish bones, since a count of individual bones within the crania would be purely arbitrary.

Fig. 5: Complete cranium of a toothed sparus, *Dentex dentex*. Top view.

Fig. 7: Complete cranium of an unidentified species. Top view.

Fig. 6: Complete cranium of a toothed sparus, *Dentex dentex*. Side view.

Fig. 8: Complete cranium of an unidentified species. Side view.

A small percentage of the fish bones have so far been identified with the help of the comparative collection of Gulf species at the Ludwig-Maximilian University in Munich. The fragments are generally well preserved and of a certain size, perhaps due to the lack of sieving, so that smaller fragments were not detected. So although fish constitute a significant part of the faunal material from the Barbar temples, it is very probable that they originally formed a larger proportion of the faunal material.

The fish which have been identified are well known from the area today and are also found at other sites in Bahrain from this period as part of the ordinary household waste (Uerpmann & Van Neer 1994). Fish bones have also been recovered from other Dilmun temples on Bahrain. At Saar, burnt fish bones have been found, left *in situ* on the altar (see Crawford 1997).

The group of fish bones includes two complete crania (see figs. 5-8). They derive from a single locus just outside the oval platform wall, and the locus contains at least two different fish species, along with two sheep or goats of a very young age. These were, as indicated by the find of the two complete crania and several vertebrae, still in anatomical articulation, probably deposited in the ground intact and with the flesh still on the bones.

Fig. 9: Two complete cleitra of narrow-barred Spanish mackerel displaying signs of hyperostosis.

13 fragmentary fish bones reveal traces of hyperostosis or excessive ossification. This condition is described for a number of species and may be related to age and metabolism. However, it is a very poorly understood condition, and it does not appear to influence the vitality of the afflicted fish (von den Driesch 1994). Among the 13 fragments found are five fragments identified as suborbital of unknown species, and five fragments were identified as cleithrum from the narrow-barred Spanish mackerel. The last three fragments displaying signs of hyperostosis are of unknown origin.

	Barbar Temple			Qala'at al-Bahrain, Excavation 520			Qala'at al-Bahrain, Excavation 519			Saar Settlement		
	N	W	%	N	W	%	N	W	%	N	W	%
Cattle *Bos taurus*	772	6320	84.9	430	6483	48.6	346	5180	44.7	28	571	25.2
Sheep *Ovis aries*	50	352	4.7	214	1764	13.2	226	1771	15.3	67	442	19.5
Goat *Capra hircus*	20	106	1.4	129	642	4.8	89	430	3.7	76	256	11.3
Sheep/goat *Ovis/Capra*	178	664	8.9	1533	4448	33.4	1552	4218	36.4	234	994	43.9
Total	1020	7442	99.9	2306	13337	100.0	2213	11599	100.1	405	2263	99.9

Table 10: Comparison of Barbar cattle – sheep/goat distribution with other contemporaneous Gulf sites

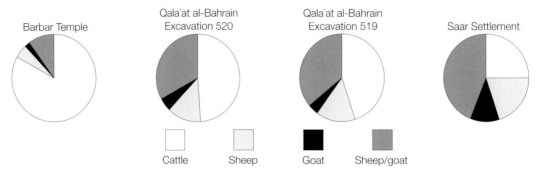

Fig. 10: Distribution of cattle, sheep and goat for Barbar and contemporaneus sites.

Comparison with other Dilmun sites

The weight of identified bones of cattle, sheep and goat from the Barbar temples display some striking differences relative to that of other contemporaneous sites from Bahrain (see table 10 and fig. 10). The distributions chosen for comparison are two from Qala'at al-Bahrain, the capital of eastern Arabia (*Dilmun*) (Uerpmann 1994 and 1997). Excavation 519 represents a public area of monumental architecture and Excavation 520 represents smaller private buildings. The third distribution is from Saar, a village or small town (Dobney 1994). Although there is no direct link between the ratio of meat on the bones and the weight of the fragments, the weight does give a better impression of the actual importance of each species

At Barbar, cattle dominate with 83% of the weight, and sheep and goat represent only 17%. At Qala'at al-Bahrain cattle are reduced to 45% for Excavation 519 and 49% for Excavation 520. Instead, goat and sheep dominates slightly, with 51% for area 520 and 55% for area 519. At Saar, the percentage of cattle is reduced even further to 25%, and sheep and goat dominate, with 75%.

That more cattle than goat and sheep were consumed at Qala'at al-Bahrain than at Saar may be explained by a higher status and greater wealth of the inhabitants of the capital than of the village, with reference to beef often being considered as a better quality meat compared to mutton or goat's meat. In line with this argumentation, the dominance of cattle at the Barbar temples can be explained by assuming that temple consumption required the highest quality possible. Alternatively, one might

suggest that cattle had a special significance in the cult of the temple, perhaps being closely related to one of the gods worshipped there or merely as a symbol of force or divinity. Both explanations seem plausible, considering the copper bull's head found at the temple itself and also the known use of cattle as a symbol in the Dilmun, Mesopotamian and Indus iconography.

It is worth mentioning that cattle appear to be of a larger size at the Barbar temples than what is recorded from Qala'at al-Bahrain. This is also the case for the goat bones, but not for the sheep bones, which are of equal size or slightly smaller. That sacrificial animals were specially selected for their age, size and exterior is known from the study of faunal material from other religious buildings, such as the Maussolleion at Halikarnasos (Aaris-Sørensen 1981). In contrast to the faunal material from a normal household, where the bones represent a more complete picture of a smaller population, the faunal material from a religious building can be a selection from a larger population or perhaps a selection originating from several different populations. Often they represent the best part of the population in the respect that only the better animals were suitable for sacrifice, and thereby the faunal material can give the impression of a larger size of animals.

This could perhaps also be supported by the age distribution for cattle, sheep and goat, as there seems to be a lack of older animals, seen in a normal population of breeding domesticated animals. Also the general age distribution for the three species is less dispersed than what is normally seen for a population of breeding animals.

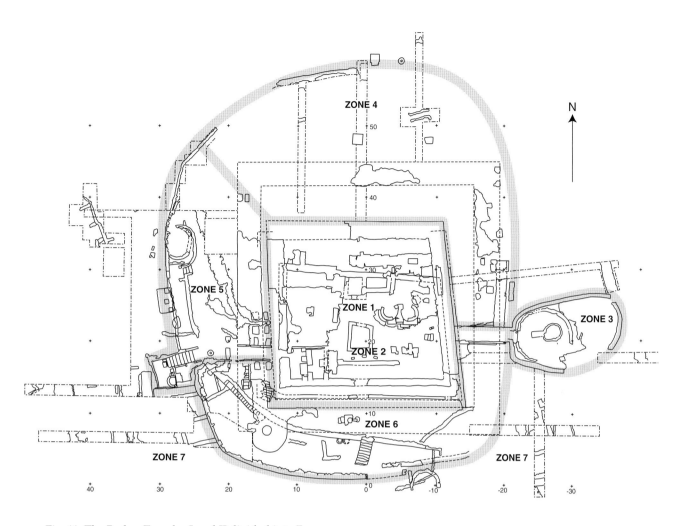

Fig. 11: The Barbar Temples I and II divided into 7 zones.

Spatial analysis

In order to detect possible spatial differences in the distribution of the faunal material, the bones securely dated to Temples I and II were divided into seven zones of origin (fig. 11). The preservation of the temple architecture is such that it allows a spatial division of the site. The material from Temples I and II was amalgamated, mainly due to the great similarity in architecture of the two temple phases, and in order to increase the volume of material for analysis.

Zone 1: The foundation layers of Temple I (8 loci)
Zone 2: The central platforms of Temples I and II (13 loci)
Zone 3: The Eastern Court of Temple II (11 loci)
Zone 4: The northern part of the oval platforms of Temples I and II (3 loci)
Zone 5: The western part of the oval platforms of Temples I and II (3 loci)
Zone 6: The southern part of the oval platforms of Temples I and II (14 loci)
Zone 7: The area outside the oval platforms (16 loci)

	Cattle Bos taurus	Sheep Ovis aries	Goat Capra hircus	Sheep/Goat Ovis/Capra	Socotra Cormorant Phalacrocorax nigrogularis	Fish	Unidentified	Total amount
Area 1 – The foundation layers								
Number	24	5	3	9	-	11	8	60
Weight	223	38	4	49	-	21	6	341
Area 2 – The central platform								
Number	19	5	3	19	-	8	57	113
Weight	230	42	4	80	-	22	100	495
Area 3 – The eastern court								
Number	51	9	6	50	-	50	168	334
Weight	901	70	42	165	-	58	233	1469
Area 4 – The northern oval platform								
Number	289	1	-	6	-	8	668	980
Weight	912	1	-	12	-	3	1089	2063
Area 5 – The western oval platform								
Number	25	3	2	14	-	17	41	102
Weight	266	23	17	122	-	53	95	576
Area 6 – The southern oval platform								
Number	73	3	1	14	1	8	58	158
Weight	821	46	10	58	0	23	106	1064
Area 7 – Outside the oval platform								
Number	145	5	4	7	-	31*	118	310
Weight	2008	45	13	30	-	747	235	3078

* In this category two complete crania have been added, each counted only as a single fragment.

Table 11: The distribution of number and weight (in grammes) of the bones from Temples I and II

The results of the division (see table 11) are shown both in numbers and in weight. The total amount of bones is not directly comparable, due to the differences in the amount of soil excavated from each area.

There is a general similarity between the bone samples from all seven zones, including the foundation layers, but some differences may be pointed out.

The amount of faunal material from the central platform is low, considering that the area was almost completely excavated. The low number and weight of the bones may be due to the probable cultic function of this particular area, where special attention was invested in order to keep it clean. This would not only limit the amount of bones found here, but also reduce the general size of the fragments.

The Eastern Court was completely and very carefully excavated. The number of bones found here is thus high and it is therefore of interest that apart from three fragments from the diaphysis of a radius (one from sheep or goat and two from cattle) all bones are either from the distal part of the leg (metapodium or carpal/tarsal bones) or from the mandible or the cranium of the animals, i.e. parts of the body which carry very little meat. This supports the interpretation of the Eastern Court as the primary place for butchering the sacrificial animals.

The northern part of the oval platform is the least excavated zone with only three loci, but it has the highest number and weight of bones. Furthermore, over 65% of these bones are white-burnt in contrast to the other loci, where only an occasional fragment or two show signs of slight burning. The burning is the main reason there are so many unidentified fragments, as it has caused extreme fragmentation. It is uncertain what has taken place in this area, but a parallel could perhaps be drawn to structures found at the Oval Temple in Khafaje (Delougaz 1940 p. 34-37) and at the Enlil temple in Nippur (McCrown et al. 1967 p. 30), where there appear to be structures designed for either disposal of temple refuse by severe burning or for food offering, although this option seems less likely, considering the extreme heat used. The special care taken for the disposal of certain types of temple refuse is known from other parts of the Middle East (see Wright 1987).

The zone outside the oval platform contains a significant number of fish bones. This is due to a single locus near the southeastern corner of the oval platform. Although no further information about the locus is available, the bones suggest that we are dealing with a deposit of some sort. The fish found here included two complete heads of a rather large size (see figs. 5-8) and several vertebrae still in anatomical articulation, both suggesting that the animals were positioned whole and with the flesh still on the bones. Also in the same locus are four bones from a very young sheep or goat, probably only a few days old. Aside from a single other bone, these are the only bones from individuals of this age.

Appendix 2. Analysis of Wood from the Barbar Temple

by Margareta Tengberg

Introduction

Several wood samples were collected during the excavations of the temple complex at Barbar. They have been studied from an anatomical point of view in order to identify the ligneous species used at the site. The results presented in this report are the first concerning wood from Barbar. However, larger quantities of charred wood samples have previously been studied from the neighbouring sites of Saar (Gale 1994) and Qal'at al-Bahrain (Tengberg & Lombard 2001), providing a first picture of the vegetation and the wood exploitation in the northern part of the island, from the Bronze age until the Achaemenid period.

The wood samples and their identification

The largest sample, consisting of 16 fragments, came from the pool, i.e. a stone-built chamber enclosing a fresh water spring to the west of the main temple building (sample no. 517.AON, area XVI 1960). These fragments were retrieved from a sandy layer at level c. 4.50. Their origin cannot be established with certainty but they might have belonged to a superstructure of wood, originally covering the well chamber.

The preservation of organic material in this context seems to be due to the more or less constant state of humidity of the sediments – and indeed the excavators noted that the wood was found below the present water-table – preventing the decay by micro-organisms such as fungi and bacteria. The structure of the wood, even though strongly compressed, has not been the subject to other types of alterations, such as mineralisation or carbonisation.

Another sample consisted of a single fragment of mineralised wood extracted from one of the numerous copper plates that seem to have been attached by nails onto wooden objects, posts, sculptures or the like, ornamenting the exterior of the temple (sample no. 517.EC). Several other copper sheets were searched for preserved wood fragments but only this one produced a piece that was sufficiently large to be analysed.

The identification of the samples was done with the help of a reflecting light microscope, with magnifications varying from ×50 to ×800. The anatomical structure of the wood, characteristic for each species, was observed in three planes (transversal, tangential and radial) and compared to modern specimens from the reference collection of the *Maison de l'Archéologie* at Nanterre and to descriptions in wood anatomical atlases (Fahn *et al.* 1986, Jagiella & Kürschner 1987, Neumann *et al.* 2000).

Identification of the fragments from the pool (517.AON) was rendered difficult by the partial collapse (or compression) of their cellular structure. Still, two types of wood could be differentiated: one belonging to the *Ziziphus* genus of the Rhamnaceae or Buckthorn family and another belonging to the Salicaceae or Willow family.

The wood of the *Ziziphus* species has a diffuse vessel arrangement, with vessels being solitary or joined in radial multiples of 2-3 cells. The rays, square and sligthly heterocellular in the radial plane, are typically uni-seriate (and very rarely bi-seriate). Parenchyma is scarce and mainly vasicentric. On the basis of the wood anatomy, an unequivocal distinction between the two *Ziziphus* species indigenous to Bahrain, *Z. nummularia* (Burm.f.) Wight & Arn. and *Z. spina-christi* (L.) Willd, cannot be done (Fahn *et al.* 1986).

The second taxa has large, polygonal inter-vessel pits, characteristic of species belonging to the Salicaceae family. The rays are narrow, mostly uni-seriate and presents rather a homocellular structure in the radial plane. This last characteristic enables us to attribute this wood to poplar (*Populus*) rather than to willow (*Salix*) for which the rays are heterocellular.

In the case of the mineralised wood (517.EC), the small size of the fragment and its mediocre state of preservation did not permit a precise identification.

Due to the presence of vessels, fibres and wooden rays, we can nevertheless be certain that we deal here with a hardwood, *i.e.* a species belonging the Dicotyledonae group of the angiosperms (flowering plants). Thus, we can exclude the presence of a softwood/coniferous taxa, such as pine tree or cedar, or a Monocotyledonae, such as date palm.

Discussion

Ziziphus spina-christi (jujuba or Christ's thorn in English, *sidr* in Arabic) is one of the most common indigenous tree species in Bahrain. Its fruits, yellow to orange at maturity, are much appreciated in the whole arid Middle East and are often sold at local markets. The smaller and shrubby *nummularia* species also produces edible drupes, similar to those of *spina-christi* but smaller in size and less fleshy. The remains of charred fruit stones found at many archaeological sites in eastern Arabia show that *Ziziphus* fruits were consumed in the region at least since the Neolithic (Costantini & Audisio 2001, Tengberg 2003).

The wood of the jujuba tree, hard and resistant, is appreciated for tools, furniture and construction elements. It is thus not surprising if this type of wood was chosen for the construction of the roof of the pool. Charred remains of *Ziziphus* wood are common on archaeological sites in the Gulf region, especially in the Oman peninsula where this taxa seems to have constituted a main element in the vegetation cover (Tengberg 2002). In Bahrain, jujuba wood has been identified from Achaemenid and Seleucid levels at Qal'at al-Bahrain (Tengberg & Lombard 2002).

The presence of poplar wood at Barbar is more problematic. The only poplar species that grows in the hot parts of the Middle East is the Euphrates poplar (*Populus euphratica*) but it is not known to be indigenous to Bahrain or to the Arabian peninsula. Poplar was also identified from Kassite levels at Qal'at al-Bahrain (*idem*). Could this hydrophilous species have been introduced to Bahrain and planted near sources and irrigation canals? Or was its wood imported from other parts of the Middle East, for example from Mesopotamia where poplar trees commonly grew along the great rivers and their tributaries? For the moment, there seems to be no straightforward answer to this question but if poplar wood was to be identified in larger quantities at sites in Bahrain, it might indicate that the species was of a particular importance to the Dilmunites, either symbolically or as a raw material.

In the Middle East, poplar wood is frequently used for construction work. The long and straight stems are particularly well-suited for making posts and beams.

Conclusion

The limited number of fragments studied (<20) and their relatively bad state of preservation have allowed the identification of two taxa only. One of these, *Ziziphus*, is indigenous to Bahrain while the other, *Populus euphratica* Oliv., is likely to have been either introduced for cultivation or imported in the form of wood. The absence of other taxa that we know were common in Bahrain in Antiquity, such as the date palm, may be imputed to the reduced number of samples.

However, these first results show the potential for further studies of wood from Barbar. The analysis of charcoal from ritual burnings for example would be particularly interesting for reconstructing the past environment around the site.

Appendix 3. Metal Analyses

by Edward Sangmeister

The samples were taken in 1960 and the results given in a report by E. Sangmeister dated 15th of March 1961 (cf. Junghans, Sangmeister & Schröder 1960).

Barbar Identifying Lot	S.A.M. Project Analysis No.	Object Type	%Sn	%Pb	%As	%Sb	%Ag	%Ni	%Bi	%Au	%Zn	%Co	%Fe
517.YM	2650	flat axe	>10	0.18	Sp	?	0.027	0.18	0	0	0	0	0.16
	2651	flat axe	>10	0.14	Sp	0	0.031	0.17	Sp	0	0	0	0.94
	2652	flat axe	>10	0.27	0.13	?	0.020	0.24	0.007	0	0	0	~1.6
	2653	flat axe	>10	0.49	0.13	0.43?	0.024	0.29	Sp	0	0	Sp	0.041
517.AGR	2654	crescent-shaped axe	1.0	0.038	0.28	?	0.067	0.22	0.002	0	0	0	0.49
	2655	axe	0.43	0	0.67	?	0.076	0.15	0	0	0	0	0.17
517.FH	2656	ingot	0	0.086	0.68	0	0.098	0.80	Sp	0	0	0	0.064
517.FG	2657	sheet	0.019	0.041	0.20	?	0.12	0.24	<0.001	0	0.033	0	0.11
517.FG	2658	sheet	~0.01	0	0	?	0.14	0.041	Sp	0	0	0	0.076
517.FI	2659	shaft-hole adze	0	1.05	0.26	0	0.092	0.20	0	0	0	0	0.012
517.P	2660	figurine	++	0	+	?	Sp	+	Sp	0	0	0	+
517.P	2661	figurine	~10	0	0.45	?	Sp	0.57	Sp	0	0	Sp	0.11
	2662	socketed spear	0.086	0.060	0.27	0.61	0.012	1.15	0.053	0	<0.01	+	>1
517.FJ	2663	bull's head	<0.01	0.013	0.40	0.12	<0.01	0.27	<0.001	Sp	0	+	0.20
Sample 27	2666	handle	Sp	0.062	0.66	?	0.036	0.43	Sp	0	0	0	>1
517.O	2667	bird	0	0.017	0.52	0.12	0.23	0.54	0.007	0	0	0.035	0.76
517.FE	2668	socketed spear	0.019	0	0.40	0	0.018	0.65	0	0	0	0	<0.001
	2669	metal fragment	0	?	0.40	0	0.031	0.64	0.12	0	0.018	0.043	>>1
	2670	metal fragment	0	0	Sp	0	++	+	0	0	0	0	Sp
	2671	metal fragment	0	0	0.46	0	0.41	0.24	0	0	0	0	Sp
	2672	metal fragment	0	0	Sp	0	0.49	0.072	0	0	0	0	0.036
	2673	metal fragment	0	0.020	0.90	0	0.051	0.090	0	0	0	0	<0.001
	2674	metal fragment	0	0	0.62	0	0.29	0.47	0	0	0	Sp	0
	2675	metal fragment	0	0	+	0	++	++	0	0	0	Sp	+
	2676	metal fragment	0	0	0.27	0	0.42	0.30	0	0	0	0	<0.001
	2677	metal fragment	0	+	+	0	++	++	0	0	0	0	+
	2678	metal fragment	0	0.022	0.74	0	0.019	0.078	0.020	0	0	Sp	>1
	2679	metal fragment	0	0.012	0.31	?	0.53	0.78	0	0	0	Sp	<0.001
	2680	metal fragment	0	<0.01	0.38	?	0.31	0.094	Sp	Sp	0	0	<0.001
	2681	metal fragment	Sp	Sp	0.38	?	0.020	0.065	Sp	0	0	0	0.006
	2682	metal fragment	0	0	0.37	0	0.23	0.20	0	0	0	0	0.002
	2683	metal fragment	0.010	0.064	0.26	?	0.10	0.24	<0.001	Sp	Sp	0	0.23

Barbar Identifying Lot	S.A.M. Project Analysis No.	Object Type	%Sn	%Pb	%As	%Sb	%Ag	%Ni	%Bi	%Au	%Zn	%Co	%Fe
	2684	metal fragment	0	0	0.60	0	0.10	0.20	0	0	0	0	0.002
	2685	metal fragment	0	0	0.54	0	0.033	0.34	0	0	0	0	0
	2686	metal fragment	0	0	Sp	0	0.16	0.18	0	0	0	0	Sp
	2687	metal fragment	0	0	Sp	0	+	+	0	0	0	0	Sp
	2688	metal fragment	0	~0.01	0.63	0	0.28	0.28	Sp	0	0	Sp	0.002
	2689	metal fragment	0	0	0.82	0	0.24	0.16	0	0	0	0	0
	2690	metal fragment	Sp	0.045	1.1	?	0.13	0.25	<0.001	0	0	0	0.005
	2691	metal fragment	Sp	Sp	0.69	?	0.39	0.12	<0.001	0	0	Sp?	0.014
	2692	metal fragment	0.061	0.064	1.1	?	0.060	0.061	<0.001	Sp	0	Sp?	<0.001
	2693	metal fragment	Sp	0	+	0	+	+	0	0	0	0	Sp
	2694	metal fragment	-	-	-	-	-	-	-	-	-	-	-
	2695	metal fragment	0	0	+	?	+	+	0	0	0	0	Sp
	2696	metal fragment	0	0	0.63	?	0.10	0.32	<0.001	0	0	Sp	<0.001
	2697	metal fragment	0	0	0.73	0	0.22	0.40	0	0	0	0	0.066
	2698	metal fragment	0	Sp	1.95	0	0.21	0.5	0.009	0	0	0	++
	2699	metal fragment	0	Sp	0.18	0	0.23	0.1	0	0	0	0	++
	2700	metal fragment	0.04	0.093	1.55	0	0.059	Sp	0.008	0	0	0	+
	2701	metal fragment	0	0	0.17	0	0.23	0.36	0	0	0	0	+
	2702	metal fragment	0	Sp	1.1	Sp	0.23	0.37	0.003	0	0	0.056	+
	2703	metal fragment	0.04	0.03	0.19	~0.03	0.051	0.1	Sp	0	0	0	+
	2704	metal fragment	Sp	~0.02	0.37	0	0.3	0.071	0	0	0	0	+
	2705	metal fragment	0	0	0.69	0	0.67	1.1	0	0	0	0.081	++
	2706	metal fragment	0	0	0.34	0	0.25	0.23	0	0	0	0	+
	2707	metal fragment	0	0.11	2.05	0	0.041	0.67	0	0	0	0	++
	2708	metal fragment	0	0.03	0.36	0	0.61	0.17	0	0	0	0	+
	2709	metal fragment	0	0	1.22	0	0.77	0.34	0	0	0	0	+
	2710	metal fragment	<0.01	0.05	0.84	~0.03	0.16	0.27	Sp	0	0	0.028	+
	2711	metal fragment	0	0.13	0.6	Sp	~0.01	0.84	0.014	0	0	0	+
	2712	metal fragment	0	Sp	0.18	0	0.23	0.068	0	0	0	0	+
	2713	metal fragment	0	Sp	0.29	~0.05	0.1	0.32	Sp	0	0	0	+
	2714	metal fragment	0.088	0	0.96	0	<0.01	0.18	0	0	0	0	+
	2715	metal fragment	0	0	0.32	0	0.06	0.33	0	0	0	0	+
	2716	metal fragment	0	0	0.56	0	1.35	0.35	0	0	0	0	Sp
	2717	metal fragment	Sp	0	1.3	Sp	0.017	0.43	0	0	0	0.033	+
	2718	metal fragment	0.24	0	0.72	0	<0.01	0.24	0	0	0	0	+
	2719	metal fragment	0	~0.03	0.37	Sp	0.14	0.15	0	0	0	0	+
	2720	metal fragment	Sp	0	0.25	Sp	Sp	0.12	0	0	0	0	+
	2721	metal fragment	Sp	Sp	+	0	+	0	Sp	0	0	0	Sp
	2722	metal fragment	0	0	0.96	0	<0.01	0.19	0	0	0	0	+
	2723	metal fragment	0	0	0.68	0	0.077	0.23	0	0	0	0	+
	2724	metal fragment	0	Sp	1.02	0	1.5	0.13	0.017	0	0	0	+
	2725	metal fragment	0	0	0.65	0	0.087	0.4	0	0	0	0	+
	2726	metal fragment	Sp	0	Sp	0	Sp	0.53	0.03	0	0	0	++

Appendix 4. Metal Analyses

by Dennis Heskel[1]

Metallographic analyses : Objects

517.A, rod (fig. 689). A cross-section of the rod was sampled. It is roughly rectangular with rounded corners. It has outer layers of the common corrosion products. The metal is reddish. There is extensive intergranular corrosion present which has outlined small equiaxed grains with numerous slip bands. There are slightly distorted spherical inclusions of copper oxide throughout the section. There is only one phase visible.

The section when etched with $FeCl_3$, contains small equiaxed grains with numerous twins and slip bands. The average grain size is 1.4 microns by point count analysis.

Spectrographic analysis indicates the bar is a pure copper with 0.8 Pb and traces of other elements as impurities, see below, p. 33.

The bar was made by hammering and annealing a cast piece. It was cold-worked after its last anneal.

517.Q, rod (fig. 697). A partial cross-section of the splayed end was sampled. In the as-polished section, there is extensive intergranular corrosion. This corrosion outlines an as-cast dendritic structure. There are spherical inclusions of copper oxide present, some of which have a lamellar structure. When etched with $FeCl_3$, the section contains an as-cast dentritic structure.

Spectrographic analysis indicates that this bar is a very pure copper with traces of other elements as impurities, see below, p. 33.

517.AP, nail (fig. 728). A cross-section from the point was taken. It is very corroded and has outer layers of the common corrosion products. It is square with little deformation visible. There is some directionality to the inclusions, which may indicate that the nail has been hammered.

When etched with $FeCl_3$, the section contains some very small equiaxed grains. There are numerous slip bands and a few twins present. The nail has been extensively cold-worked after the final anneal. Because it is so corroded, there are no phases visible, although spectrographic analysis indicates that this nail is made of a copper-low arsenic-low nickel metal with 1.6% As and 1.5% Ni, with traces of other elements, see below, p. 33. It has an average hardness of 130 VHN.

A cross-section of the head of the nail is square. It has outer layers of the common corrosion products. In the as-polished section, there are numerous copper oxide inclusions, some of which represent the eutectoid and some of which are slightly hammered after the last anneal.

When etched with $FeCl_3$, the section contains linear, straight flow lines that indicate that the nail has been compressed by hammering from a cast bar. There are elongated, deformed grains parallel to the direction of the flow lines. There are also numerous twins and some slip bands. This section has an average hardness of 122.5 VHN.

The nail was made by hammering and annealing a bar of copper-low arsenic-low nickel metal. The head of the nail was slightly cold-worked after the final anneal. The point was more extensively cold-worked after the last anneal to harden the tip.

517.BF, a curved rod (fig. 729). Section A is a cross-section of the bar. It has a thin outer layer of the common corrosion products. In the as-polished section, there is some intergranular corrosion present which has outlined some equiaxed grains and slip bands. There are small spherical copper oxide inclusions evenly spaced throughout the section. The metal is very pale in colour.

---

[1] The following analyses are excerpted from a report entitled *Corpus of Metal Objects of the Barbar Temple*, dated 1984. It has not been possible to establish contact with the author, and the text has been slightly edited.

The section when etched with FeCl$_3$ has large equiaxed grains in the center. The grains average 7.7 microns in size as measured by point count analysis. The grains are smaller towards the outer edge of the sample, and those along the outside edge are quite small. There are a large number of twins throughout the section. There are also a lot of slip bands present, particularly along the outer edge, and a few in the center of the sample. The piece was hammered and annealed with a final cold working after the last anneal. The outer edge is regular in shape and there are no cavities or evidence of the metal having been folded over. The hammering and annealing were probably to finish shaping of the object from an essentially as-cast shape. This section has an average hardness of 125 VHN.

Section B is a transverse sample of the bar. It has thin outer layers of the common corrosion products and is slightly and regularly curved. There is extensive intergranular corrosion which has outlined small equiaxed grains and some slip bands. There are small slightly elongated copper oxide inclusions throughout the section and parallel to the outer edges of the piece.

When etched with FeCl$_3$, this section also has larger equiaxed grains in the center than along the edge. There are a number of twins and a few bent twins visible. There are also a few slip bands present.

Spectrographic analysis indicates that this piece was made of copper-high tin-low arsenic metal with > 5% Sn, 1.1% As, and traces of other elements, see below. The piece retains essentially its as-cast shape with some finishing cold working and annealing.

517.DX, rod (fig. 731). A cross-section from near the broken end is circular. It has outer layers of the common corrosion products. The metal is reddish. The as-polished section has extensive intergranular corrosion and there is a cavity in the center. The corrosion has outlined medium-sized equiaxed grains which are slightly deformed and a number of slip bands. There are a number of slightly distorted spherical inclusions of copper oxide.

The central cavity appears to have been formed by the folding over of an as-cast bar by hammering to form the as-cast pin.

The presence of the cavity indicates extensive hammering to form the pin. The slip bands and deformed equiaxed grains suggest the pin was cold-worked after its last anneal.

When the section was etched with FeCl$_3$, it was found to contain medium-sized equiaxed grains and a number of twins. No flow lines were visible, although the cavity and elongated inclusions suggest extensive cold working and annealing.

A cross-section through the head of the pin was analysed. It is circular and has outer layers of the common corrosion products. There is extensive intergranular corrosion, which has outlined medium-sized equiaxed grains and numerous slip bands. There is a central cavity that suggests the pin was made by folding over a rectangular in-section bar by hammering. There are numerous elongated inclusions which form broken "stringers". These elongated inclusions are located in direction consistent with the circular hammering of a bar to form the pin.

While the section is very corroded, when etched with FeCl$_3$, there are medium-sized equiaxed grains and a few twins visible. No flow lines are present.

Spectrographic analysis indicates that this pin is made of pure copper with 0.25% As, and traces of other elements, see below. This object was formed by the folding over by extensive hammering and annealing of an as-cast rectangular bar to form the circular cross-section pin.

517.FB, dagger (fig. 734). A partial transverse section at the end of the tang was mounted. The section is totally corroded.

A partial transverse section of the tip of the blade was examined. It is very corroded with the common copper corrosion products visible. The metal is reddish in colour. Intergranular corrosion has outlined large equiaxed grains. There are spherical inclusions of copper oxide throughout the section. It is too corroded to etch.

Spectrographic analysis indicates that this spearhead is made of pure copper with 0.35% As, 0.4% Sn, and traces of other elements, see below.

517.FD, 3 fragments of rod (fig. 735). Sample A is possibly a cross-section of the tip area. It is square with rounded corners. It has outer layers of the common corrosion products. The metal is reddish and there are a lot of copper oxide inclusions, some of which are elongated by hammering. The direction of the inclusions indicates that the corners were rounded by hammering, probably in the shaping and hardening of the point.

There were no flow lines visible when the section was etched with FeCl$_3$. The etched section contains medium size equiaxed grains with twins present. The average grain size is 3.5 microns as measured by point count analysis. There were no slip bands visible. The pin was hammered and annealed, possibly to form the point. It was not cold-worked after the final anneal and thus not hardened for use. This section has an average hardness of 86 VHN.

A cross-section of the head of the pin, Sample B, is square, with two corners rounded. In the as-polished section, there are numerous small copper oxide inclusions that are generally spherical except near a cavity in the center of the section where the inclusions are elongated, following the direction of the cavity. The cavity appears to have been made by folding the metal over by hammering to form the head of the pin.

When etched with K_2CrO_7 there are a few faint flow lines visible that suggest that the hammering of the metal took place from one side of the as-cast bar to form the head. The hammering was from both upper and lower sides of this bar, and the cavity formed when these met. The corners formed by the hammering are more rounded.

When etched with $FeCl_3$, the section has very small equiaxed grains and numerous twins visible. No slip bands are present. The head of the pin was extensively hammered and annealed into its final form but was not extensively cold-worked after the final anneal. This section has an average hardness of 155 VHN.

Spectrographic analysis indicates that this pin was made of a copper-low arsenic metal with 1% As and traces of other impurities, see below.

517.FE, spearhead (fig. 736). A partial cross-section of the blade edge was taken. The metal is reddish. There is a cavity in the central part of the section, now filled with corrosion. This cavity may have been formed by shrinkage of the metal in the cooling of the casting. There are numerous spherical inclusions of copper oxide throughout the section.

The section was etched with $FeCl_3$. The etched section contains very large grains. Intergranular corrosion has also outlined large equiaxed grains. There are a few twins visible. The blade of the spearhead has probably been slightly hammered and annealed into its final shape. It has not been cold-worked after the final anneal.

Spectrographic analysis by Kennecott Copper Corporation and the S.A.M. project indicate that the spearhead is made of pure copper. The analysis by the S.A.M. project indicates the presence of 0.4% As and 0.65 Ni as minor trace elements, see above, p. 19. The analysis by Kennecott Copper shows only 0.02% As and 0.08 Ni as impurities, see below.

A partial cross-section of the end of the socket was examined. This section is very corroded and there are a few small white inclusions present, probably silver. There are large spherical inclusions of copper oxide through the section.

When etched with $FeCl_3$, the section contains large equiaxed grains which indicate the spearhead was annealed and cooled slowly. There are twins visible. Intergranular corrosion has outlined large equiaxed grains. The socket was slightly hammered and annealed into its final shape from the original casting. It was not cold-worked after the final anneal.

517.FN, sheet. A partial transverse section from the edge of the sheet was taken. In the as-polished section, it has a thick layer of cuprite. There are numerous spherical and some elongated inclusions of copper oxide present. Intergranular corrosion has outlined some medium-sized equiaxed grains which are slightly distorted.

The section was etched with $FeCl_3$. The etched section contains medium-sized equiaxed grains. There are a few twins visible.

Spectrographic analysis indicates that this sheet is made of pure copper with traces of other elements as impurities, see below.

The sheet has been hammered and annealed to its final shape. It was not cold-worked after the last anneal.

517.FN, nail with some sheet attached (fig. 704). A transverse section of the point was taken. It has thin outer layers of the common corrosion products. The point is deformed and irregular in shape. The sides taper regularly to the point and are slightly deformed. There are numerous inclusions of copper oxide. These inclusions are slightly elongated parallel to the sides of the nail. There is little intergranular corrosion present, most of it located in the point area.

When the section is etched with $FeCl_3$, there are deformed and elongated grains present. The average grain size is 3.5 microns as estimated by point count analysis. There are numerous twins and slip bands present. Only one phase is visible and spectrographic analysis indicates that this nail is made of pure copper with 0.4% As, 0.5% Fe, and traces of other elements as impurities. This section has an average hardness of 166 VHN.

A cross-section of the body is square. It has thin outer layers of the common corrosion products. The corners are rounded. There is little intergranular corrosion present. There are numerous slightly elongated inclusions of copper oxide present in the as-polished section. These inclusions show directionality near the corners of the section and indicate the hammering of the edges. The inclusions in the center of the section are spherical and not distorted.

The section, when etched with $FeCl_3$, contains some flow lines, particularly around the outer edges of the nail. These flow lines indicate that the nail has been hammered in a circular direction but has not been extensively cold-worked. The etched section also contains large equiaxed grains which are deformed along the outer edge of the sample. There are also numerous twins and slip bands present throughout the section, with more slip bands along the outer edge. This section has an average hardness of 158 VHN.

The nail has been hammered and annealed from a rod of cast copper. It has been cold-worked in a circular direction after the final anneal.

A transverse section of the head of the nail and the sheet metal the nail was hammered into was examined. All the pieces have thin outer layers of the common corrosion product. It appears that a hole, slightly larger than the body of the nail, was punched into the sheet metal from the outside edge of the sheet before the nail was hammered in. The sheet metal is bent a considerable amount inwards. There is a gap on both sides between the nail and the sheet metal. The nail does show some distortion along the outer edges of the surface, probably from being hammered into another surface. This deformation is visible in the as-polished section from the directionality of the inclusions and location of intergranular corrosion.

The sheet metal also has numerous elongated inclusions of copper oxide. These inclusions are particularly elongated in the area and direction of the punched hole. The head of the nail is flattened and quite deformed by hammering. All pieces have little intergranular corrosion.

The sheet metal and the head of the nail were etched with $FeCl_3$. The etched section contains flow lines that indicate that the nail was compressed by hammering lengthwise. This probably occurred in manufacture of the nail, not use. There are also some very large equiaxed grains which are slightly distorted from cold work after the final anneal. There are numerous twins and slip bands visible throughout the section.

The nail has been hammered and annealed from a cast rod of pure copper. It has been cold-worked after the final anneal. It has an average hardness of 153 VHN.

The sheet metal has large equiaxed grains in the etched section. There are numerous twins but no visible slip bands. It was not worked after its final anneal, which would have made it easier to punch holes and hammer nails through the sheet. The grains in the area where the hole was punched in the sheet are distorted but do not contain any slip bands. The sheet appears to be made of pure copper, which is softer than the copper alloys. It has an average hardness of 98 VHN.

517.FN, chisel? (fig. 705). A cross-section of the head shows thick outer layers of the common copper corrosion products. There are elongated and distorted inclusions of copper oxide visible.

The section was etched with $FeCl_3$. The etched section contains small- to medium-sized equiaxed grains. There are numerous twins present throughout the section. The copper oxide inclusions are elongated and broken up like "stringers". There are flow lines present that run parallel to the width of

the head of the chisel. The head was compressed by hammering to make it wider. The chisel has been hammered and annealed to make its final shape from an as-cast bar. It was not cold-worked after the last anneal.

A cross-section from the tip was examined. It has thick outer layers of the common copper corrosion products. There are very elongated inclusions of copper oxide throughout the section. Intergranular corrosion has outlined a few small equiaxed grains. The section is roughly rectangular but quite deformed.

The section, when etched with $FeCl_3$, contains some flow lines. The flow lines run parallel to the width of the chisel and indicate the tip was compressed by hammering to make it wider and thinner. There are a number of twins visible but no slip bands.

Spectrographic analysis indicates that the chisel is made of a copper-low arsenic metal with 1.5% As, with 0.2% Ag, 0.7% Fe, 0.45% Ni, 0.2% Pb, 0.45% Sn and traces of other elements as impurities, see below. It was hammered and annealed to form its final shape from an as-cast bar. It was not cold-worked after the final anneal, and even the tip was not edge-hardened.

517.FN, knife? (fig. 706). A section through the point is corroded. There appears to be a cavity that runs the width of the section. The as-polished section contains numerous elongated copper oxide inclusions. The elongated inclusions run parallel to the top and bottom of the blade, indicating that the blade was hammered to make it thinner and wider. There is some intergranular corrosion present.

When the section is etched with $FeCl_3$, flow lines are visible that are parallel with the top and bottom sides of the blade. This further indicates the hammering of the blade to make it thinner and wider. There are also numerous slip bands, twins, and some bent twins present. There are medium-sized equiaxed grains visible. This knife blade has been extensively hammered and cold-worked after the last anneal. This section has an average hardness of 169 VHN. The blade was therefore edge-hardened, and this may indicate that the piece was used, rather than purely a votive offering. Spectrographic analysis indicates that the knife was made of pure copper with 0.35% As, 0.3% Ni, 0.1% Sn and traces of other elements as impurities, see below.

A cross-section of the part of the tang flattened for hafting is roughly rectangular, with a pronounced taper towards the edges. There is a small cavity in the center of this section. There are numerous small elongated inclusions of copper oxide in the as-polished section. These inclusions are elongated parallel to the sides of the tang. The knife tang was hammered to make it wider and thinner like the blade.

The section contains flow lines parallel to the top and bottom sides of the tang when etched with $FeCl_3$. There are also thin elongated broken up "stringers" of copper oxide parallel to the flow lines. There are medium-sized equiaxed grains visible. There are numerous slip bands, some twins, and a few bent twins present in the section. It has an average hardness of 166 VHN.

This knife was made of pure copper, and it has been extensively hammered into its final shape from an as-cast bar. It has been cold-worked after the final anneal and the blade edge-hardened.

517.YM, axe (fig. 737). A cross-section of the butt end is triangular with a tapered and rounded edge. The section is heavily corroded, and the metal is pale in colour. In the as-polished section, intergranular corrosion has outlined small equiaxed grains with numerous slip bands. The butt end has been hammered and annealed with extensive cold working after the final anneal, possibly to shape the end for hafting the axe head.

When etched with K_2CrO_7, the section contains small equiaxed grains with numerous slip bands, and very few twins. The grain size is smaller near the edge but the slip bands are equally numerous throughout the section. The average grain size is 2.69 microns as measured by point count analysis.

A transverse section of the blade edge tapers to the edge, which is rounded and blunt. In the as-polished section, intergranular corrosion has outlined medium-sized equiaxed grains with numerous slip bands. The metal is pale in colour. There are a few copper oxide inclusions, and they are elongated parallel to the top and bottom sides of the blade. When etched with $FeCl_3$, there are medium-sized equiaxed grains with numerous slip bands visible throughout the section. The average grain size is 3.5 microns as measured by point count analysis. The grains are, however, smaller near the blade edge and there are more slip bands present in this area. There are no visible twins.

This piece has been extensively hammered after the last anneal, especially the blade edge. The edge hardening may indicate that the axe was used rather than purely for ceremonial purposes. The blade edge has an average hardness of 148 VHN.

The axe was sampled by the S.A.M. project, and this analysis indicates that the axe is made of a copper-high tin alloy with > 10% tin, see above, p. 19. This analysis conforms closely to the results obtained by Kennecott Copper Corporation. This analysis also shows that the metal was a copper-high tin alloy with 10% tin and traces of other impurities, see below.

517.ACL, ingot (fig. 674). A partial cross-section of the ingot was sampled. It has the common corrosion products in outer layers. The metal is reddish. The section retains an as-cast structure. There are numerous large spherical inclusions, some of which are copper oxide, and the rest appear to be iron sulfides and are a grey-green colour. These grey-green inclusions comprise about 7% by volume of the section. From the large size of the inclusions and large cored structure of the metal and corrosion mineral, this piece appears to have been cooled slowly. When etched with $FeCl_3$, there are two phases visible in the section: a dominant red copper phase that cooled first; and a small amount, 1-1.5% by volume, of a white phase that cooled after the red phase. This section has an average hardness of 88 VHN.

Spectrographic analysis, see below, indicates that the ingot is made of a pure copper with traces of other elements as impurities. It is in the as-cast state.

517.AEB, nail (fig. 743). A transverse section of the point was sampled. The metal is reddish. The point is very distorted, perhaps a result of the chemical cleaning. There are numerous spherical inclusions of copper oxide present. There is extensive intergranular corrosion and large cavities of "salt and pepper" corrosion present in the as-polished section.

When etched with $FeCl_3$, the section contains large distorted and elongated grains. The grains are elongated parallel with the length of the nail. There are numerous twins and slip bands visible throughout the section. The grains are slightly smaller and there are more slip bands at the tip of the nail, and the point may have been slightly edge-hardened. There are numerous small bright white inclusions, probably silver, located through the section, about 0.8% by volume. This section has an average hardness of 158 VHN.

Spectrographic analysis indicates that this nail is made of pure copper with 1% Ag, and traces of other elements as impurities, see below.

The nail has been hammered and annealed to produce its final shape from a cast rod. It has been cold-worked after the final anneal.

517.AGS, spearhead (fig. 661). Two sections were taken for analysis: a partial cross-section from the blade edge and a cross-section from one of the prongs of the tang.

A partial cross-section of the blade is rectangular with the blade edge rounded. The sample is very corroded with extensive intergranular corrosion. The chemical cleaning has removed the outer layers of corrosion. There is, however, an unusual purplish granulated "salt and pepper" corrosion product. The metal is pale in colour and there are several white phase inclusions present, possibly arsenic. There is a deep blue veined corrosion product associated with these white phases.

The blade edge is evenly rounded and somewhat deformed, although since the sample has been chemically cleaned, it is impossible to determine if the deformation is a result of use.

When the section was etched with FeCl$_3$, some directional flow lines were brought out that indicate the edge hammering of the as-cast spearhead. The flow lines probably represent the remnants of the original cored structure. There are very small equiaxed grains, which means the piece was annealed, but no twins or slip bands are visible in the small grains.

A cross-section from a folded-over prong of the tang has extensive intergranular corrosion in the as-polished section. The prong appears to have been made by hammering over a flat sheet. There are very small equiaxed grains outlined by the corrosion particularly around the bend in the metal. The rest of the section has slightly larger grains. The metal is pale in colour.

When this section is etched with FeCl$_3$, flow lines were visible at low magnification, ×50. The flow lines follow the curve of the section and indicate that the prongs of the tang were formed by folding over a piece of as-cast sheet by hammering. The flow lines retain some remnants of a cored structure with a red copper phase and a white copper-arsenic phase.

There are few visible grains in the section and they are medium in size and equiaxed. There are also a few twins present that indicate the tang was annealed. There are also a few slip bands visible, so that the tang was slightly cold-worked after its last anneal.

Spectrographic analysis of a sample from this spearhead, see below, indicated the presence of 1.6% arsenic as the only minor element. The spearhead was made by hammering and annealing a sheet made of a copper-low arsenic metal. The blade edge was work-hardened and the tang made by folding over the sheet by hammering. It appears that the prongs of the spearhead were split with a chisel and then folded over by hammering. It is possible that the butt of the blade was attached to the tang by folding the prongs over the butt edge and thus securing the blade by mechanical pressure.

517.AHD, rod fragment (fig. 686). Sample A is a cross-section from the broken end of the rod. It is square. It has the common outer layers of corrosion products. The metal is reddish. The as-polished section has a large cavity visible that runs diagonally across the entire section. The cavity indicates that the rod was made by hammering over a flat rectangular sheet to form the square bar. The corners of the section are well rounded. There are numerous elongated small copper oxide inclusions. These inclusions directionally follow the past hammering and have been reduced in size by the successive cold working and annealing sequences. Intergranular corrosion has outlined some equiaxed grains along the outer edge of the section.

When etched with FeCl$_3$, the section contains small equiaxed grains and twins. No slip bands are visible. No flow lines were present, but it appears that this rod was made by folding over a piece of sheet by a sequence of hammering and annealing. It was not cold-worked after the final anneal.

A transverse section, Sample B, was taken of the end of the rod with two prongs. Each prong is rectangular. Each has outer layers of the common corrosion products. The two prongs are separated by a cavity or space between them. Each has numerous small elongated inclusions of copper oxide. The inclusions run parallel to the length of the rod. Intergranular corrosion has outlined medium-sized equiaxed grains along the edges of each of the prongs in the as-polished sample.

The section, when etched with FeCl$_3$, contains numerous twins and a few slip bands. There are medium-sized equiaxed grains throughout the section. The elongated copper oxide inclusions are broken up like "stringers". This section has an average hardness of 141 VHN.

This rod was made by extensive hammering and annealing of two pieces of cast wire that was rectangular in section. The cold working lengthened the rod. It is puzzling, however, that there is no fold or hinge visible in the metal.

Spectrographic analysis indicates that this rod is made of pure copper with 0.7% As, 0.6% Ni, and traces of other elements as impurities, see below.

517. AHF, fragment of ingot (fig. 682). A cross-section was examined. In the as-polished section, it contains outer layers of the usual corrosion products. It retains an as-cast structure. The metal is pale. There are large spherical inclusions of copper oxide and a grey phase that is probably lead. The copper oxide inclusions form lamellar eutectoid patterns throughout the section. There are also a few inclusions of grey iron silicate. The ingot may represent an example of the last refining stage of the imported metal. The section was etched with FeCl$_3$. The etched section contains a cored structure with two phases: a red copper phase which cooled first; and, small amounts of a white phase, probably copper-arsenic, which occurs with a blue-grey veining.

517.AHI, fragment of ingot (fig. 683). A cross-section has thin outer layers of the common corrosion products. The metal is reddish. There are numerous large spheres of lead throughout the section.

The section when etched with $FeCl_3$ has large grains which indicate the piece was slow cooled. There is only one phase visible, with the lead inclusions at the grain boundaries. There are some elongated "striations" that appear to follow the same orientation as the grains.

The piece appears to be as cast and probably represents a fragment of refined metal. Spectrographic analysis of a sample from this fragment shows > 2% Pb, 0.3% As, 0.6% Ag, 0.1% Ni, 0.25% Sb, and small traces of other elements, see below. A hardness test indicates that the section has an average hardness of 132 VHN.

517.AHI, fragment probably from ingot (fig. 684). A partial transverse section was sampled and examined. The section has outer layers of the common corrosion products. In the as-polished section, the metal is pale. There is an as-cast structure with two phases present, a predominant metal phase, and, a second phase that has corroded to blue-grey mineral and that measures about 5% by volume.

There are copper oxide inclusions present that have a dentritical shape. The piece appears to be as cast. When etched with K_2CnO_7 and $FeCl_3$, the section contains an as-cast cored structure with two phases. The predominant phase is a red copper one. The second phase contains both white metallic and blue-grey mineral components. The red phase appears to have solidified first. There is about 18% of the second phase by volume as measured by the point count method of analysis.

Spectrographic analysis indicates that the ingot fragment is made of a copper-low arsenic metal with 1.3% As and traces of other elements as impurities, see below. It has an average hardness of 114 VHN.

517.AHI, fishhook? (fig. 685). A transverse section of the point and bend in the fishhook, Sample A, was taken. It has thin outer layers of the common corrosion products. In the as-polished section, there are numerous elongated copper oxide inclusions visible. These inclusions are elongated parallel to the sides of the fishhook. There is a cavity where the bend in the fishhook was made by hammering, indicating both a fairly crude job and excessive cold work. The point is regular and rounded. There is some intergranular corrosion present, particularly near the point.

The section when etched with $FeCl_3$, contains very small grains that are extensively deformed and elongated. The average grain size is 0.7 microns as estimated by point count analysis. There are numerous slip bands, twins, and bent twins present. The point has been extensively cold-worked after its last anneal. The fishhook point has been extensively hammered and annealed into shape from an as-cast bar. The bend in the body of this fishhook is caused by the cold working. This section has an average hardness of 147 VHN.

Spectrographic analysis indicates that the fishhook is made of a copper-medium arsenic-medium nickel alloy with 2% As and 2% Ni, with traces of other elements as impurities, see below. This metal is reasonably hard and lack of sufficient knowledge of its properties may also be partly responsible for the crack in the fishhook.

A cross-section of the head of the fishhook, Sample B, was examined. It is oval and has thick layers of the common corrosion products. The outer edges are deformed, probably by hammering to flatten the head. There are numerous spherical inclusions of copper present, which has outlined some very small grains which are slightly distorted.

When the section was etched with $FeCl_3$, it was found to contain very small grains, mostly equiaxed. The average grain size is 0.66 microns when estimated by point count analysis. There are numerous twins and a few slip bands visible. The head of the fishhook has also been shaped by hammering and annealing an as-cast bar, but is less worked than the point area. The head region has been slightly cold-worked after the final anneal. It has an average hardness of 142 VHN.

517.AHI, chisel? A partial transverse section of the blade edge of the chisel was sampled. It has thick outer layers of the common corrosion products. There is extensive intergranular corrosion present, which has outlined some very distorted and elongated grains. The blade edge is thin and deformed, and this piece was definitely used. There are numerous elongated inclusions throughout the section. These inclusions are elongated parallel to the length of the chisel.

The section, when etched with $FeCl_3$, contains elongated and deformed large grains particularly near the blade edge. The average grain size is 3.5 microns as measured by point count analysis. The grains are elongated parallel to the length of the chisel. There are numerous slip bands present and a few twins. It has an average hardness of 146 VHN.

Spectrographic analysis shows that this chisel is made of pure copper with 0.5% As, 0.7% Fe, 0.2% Ni, and traces of other elements as impurities, see below.

The chisel was made by hammering and annealing an as-cast bar. It has been cold-worked after the last anneal, probably to harden the blade edge. It is too corroded, however, for its hardness to be measured.

517.AHV, fragment of ingot (fig. 739). Sample A is a transverse section and is triangular. It has the common outer corrosion layers. It is heavily corroded. There are numerous spherical copper oxide inclusions throughout the section. When etched with FeCl$_3$, the section has a definite cored structure with a dominant red copper phase and less prevalent white copper-arsenic phase. The copper oxide inclusions appear to be mostly located at the interface of the two phases. There also seems to be a blue-grey arsenic-rich phase associated with the white phase. This blue phase seems to have formed a cored structure with the white phase.

A cross-section of the ingot, Sample B, is rectangular. The metal is pale in colour. The copper oxide inclusions retain an eutectic pattern and also have a well-defined lamellar structure. It has outer layers of the common corrosion products.

When etched with FeCl$_3$, a cored structure is visible. The major phase is a red copper one. There is a small amount of a white copper-arsenic phase. This phase represents 2% of the volume as estimated by point count analysis. There are small blue-grey inclusions associated with the white phase and a blue phase which retains a cored structure inside the white phase.

This fragment is in an as-cast state and represents the final refining of a copper-low arsenic metal. Spectrographic analysis indicates the presence of 1% arsenic and traces of other impurities, see below. The piece has an average hardness of 118 VHN.

517.AIB, fragment of rod (fig. 740). A transverse section of the rounded tip has outer layers of the usual corrosion products. The metal is very yellow in colour. The tip is well rounded and not deformed. There is extensive intergranular corrosion in the as-polished section, especially at the tip. The intergranular corrosion has outlined medium-sized slightly distorted equiaxed grains. There are numerous inclusions located throughout the section. Some of these inclusions are alongated. The rod has been hammered and annealed to its final shape from a cast rod. It probably was slightly cold-worked after the last anneal.

The section, when etched with FeCl$_3$, contains a few slip bands and numerous twins. There are medium- to small-sized equiaxed grains visible. The average grain size is 1.8 microns by point count analysis. There are dark grey, slightly deformed spherical lead inclusions throughout the section. These inclusions form a slightly distorted eutectic pattern.

Spectrographic analysis indicates that this rod is made of a copper-low lead-low tin-high zinc alloy with 1.1% Pb, 1.2% Sn, and more than 5% Zn, with traces of other elements as impurities. This is an alloy somewhat like brass and is known only from Tepe Hissar, Iran, in the early second millennium B.C. The rod is essentially as cast with final shaping by hammering and annealing. It was slightly cold-

worked after the final anneal. It has an average hardness of 197 VHN and is extremely hard. It probably dates to the Islamic period.

517.AJH, fragment of sheet (fig. 663). A cross-section near one end of the fragment has outer layers of the common corrosion products. The metal is reddish and there are numerous elongated copper oxide inclusions. The inclusions are oriented parallel to the top and bottom of the fragment. There is some intergranular corrosion in the section, mostly located around an indentation in the bottom of the fragment.

The section when etched with FeCl$_3$ contains large equiaxed grains with numerous twins. The average grain size is 2.08 microns as measured by point count analysis. There is only a single red phase visible. Spectrographic analysis indicates that the sheet was made of pure copper with traces of other elements, see below. There are no slip bands present, and the sheet was not cold-worked after the final anneal. This section has an average hardness of 117 VHN.

A cross-section of the other end of the fragment also has outer layers of the common corrosion products. There is extensive intergranular corrosion present, particularly near a large indentation near the edge. There are numerous elongated copper oxide inclusions. The inclusions parallel the top and bottom surfaces of the fragment.

The section was etched with FeCl$_3$. The etched section contains medium-sized equiaxed grains with numerous twins. The average grain size was 2.1 microns as measured by point count analysis. There are some broken "stringers" of copper oxide visible. There are a few slip bands and bent twins present. This section has an average hardness of 110 VHN.

This sheet was hammered and annealed from a cast bar. The working made the sheet wider and thinner. Only in one end of the fragment is there evidence of slight cold working after the final anneal, probably for final shaping.

517.AJI, a rod (fig. 665). A cross-section of the tip, Sample A, was mounted. It is extremely corroded with the common copper corrosion products present. There are small amounts of reddish metal visible throughout the section. The section is very deformed, but it is not possible to determine if this deformation is the result of working.

A cross-section of the head, Sample B, was taken. It is roughly rectangular and has outer layers of the common corrosion products. There is extensive intergranular corrosion visible which has outlined elongated and distorted grains. There are numerous elongated inclusions of copper oxide throughout the section. There are also large cavities filled with a "salt and pepper" granular corrosion.

The section was etched with FeCl$_3$. The etched section contains flow lines that are parallel to the width of the pin. These flow lines indicate that the pin was compressed by hammering to make it wider. The grains are large and very distorted. These grains are as large as 6.5 microns as measured by point count analysis. There are numerous large slip bands present in these grains. The copper oxide inclusions are also elongated parallel to the width of the section. A hardness test of the head of the pin indicates an average hardness of 152 VHN, a very hard copper. Spectrographic analysis indicates that this pin is made of a copper-low arsenic metal with 1% As, with 0.3% Sn, 0.2% Ni, 0.1% Ag and traces of other elements as impurities.

This small pin has been hammered and annealed from the as-cast bar to form its final shape. It has been extensively cold-worked after the final anneal and the pin is extremely hard. It would have been suitable for punching holes in the sheet metal or other strenuous tasks.

517.AJI, fragment of the socket of shafthole adze (fig. 664). A transverse section of the lower rim part of the socket. It has outer layers of the common corrosion products. The polished section has a visible as-cast cored structure with one of the phases present as corrosion product. There are very few small copper oxide inclusions present, and there are small grey lead inclusions visible about 1.5% by volume. The cored structure is deformed only along the rim, which indicates that the rim was slightly hammered into its final shape and along the outer side. This is a well cast piece.

When etched with FeCl$_3$, the section contains a cored structure with a small amount of a reddish phase which cooled first and a dominant white phase which has not corroded. The rim section and outer side show some deformation of the cored structure, and there are some twins localized in these areas. This section has an average hardness of 110 VHN.

The socket remains essentially in the as-cast state except for an area where slight final shaping occurred. Spectrographic analysis indicates that this adze is made of a copper-low lead alloy with 1.2% Pb and traces of other elements as impurities.

517.ALB, crescent-shaped axe? (fig. 668). A cross-section of the socket, Sample A, was examined. The section has a thick outer layer of cuprite. The metal is reddish. There is extensive intergranular corrosion present, which has outlined small equiaxed grains and some slip bands. There are numerous spherical copper oxide inclusions throughout the section. There are large cavities filled with corrosion that follow the general shape of the socket.

The section, when etched with FeCl$_3$, contains small slightly distorted equiaxed grains. There are a few twins and slip bands visible. The socket was made by hammering and annealing as-cast sheet until a tube was formed. The opening in the tube is ovoid in shape. The socket was cold-worked after the final anneal.

A partial cross-section of the blade, Sample B, was taken. It is extremely corroded and contains little metal.

Spectrographic analysis of the crescent axe indicates it is made of a copper-low tin alloy with 1% Sn and traces of other elements as impurities, see below.

517.ALD, knife? (fig. 670). A partial cross-section of the haft end was sampled. The section is almost totally corroded with what appears to be an outer strip of reddish redeposited metal and a small segment of white metal as an inclusion, possibly silver. The fold to form the haft appears regular and rounded. The end of the folded section is flat.

517.ALL, dagger (fig. 671). A partial transverse section of the haft end of the tang was taken. It is extremely corroded. The metal is reddish. There is only one phase visible, and there are spherical copper oxide inclusions present. The section is too corroded to etch.

517.AOS, ingot fragment (fig. 676). A partial cross-section of the ingot fragment was taken. In the as-polished section, there are large copper dendrites present, indicating that the ingot was cooled slowly. There are numerous large spherical inclusions of copper oxide present. There is a lot, about 50% of the volume, of a grey silicate product found in the section. There are also some small pieces of a slightly heated mineral. This mineral appears to be chalcopyrite or a complex CuFeS mineral, based on its extinction colour under polarized light. The metal visible is reddish and only one phase is visible when the section is etched with FeCl$_3$. The silicate is viscous and is primarily fayalite, Fe$_3$O$_4$, although there is some Fe$_2$O$_3$ present. There are few gas holes present in the dross, despite evidence of a lot of oxygen in the process, i.e. the fayalite and large upper oxide inclusions. There is some covellite present as small inclusions. The copper is well separated and the admixture of ore, prills, and flux appears to have been good. From this and the presence of the slightly altered chalcopyrite, the smelting temperature of this crucible was between 1,200-1,500°C.

The ingot fragment is not very pure and contains a lot of silicate material. This is most probably a result of a refining stage; the initial smelting and perhaps other refining stages took place elsewhere.

29

517.ARV, dagger (fig. 725). A partial transverse section of the tip was sampled. It is extensively corroded with thick layers of the common corrosion products. There are numerous elongated inclusions throughout the section. They are elongated parallel to the sides of the blade.

When etched with $FeCl_3$, the section contains very elongated large grains parallel to the top and bottom of the blade. There are numerous slip bands and a few twins and bent twins present.

The dagger has been hammered and annealed from an as-cast shape. It has been extensively cold-worked after the last anneal to harden the edge. Spectrographic analysis, see below, indicates that this dagger is made from a copper-low arsenic-low tin alloy with 2% As, 2.3% Sn and 0.8% Ni, 0.6% Fe, and traces of other elements as impurities. This alloy is well suited for a hard, usable dagger.

517.ARZ, bead (fig. 726). A cross-section from the curved portion of the bead was sampled. It is oval with even and regular sides. The metal is yellowish in colour. It has unusual surface corrosion products and may have been chemically cleaned. There are spherical inclusions of a number of different materials in the section, including copper oxide. There are large dark grey spherical inclusions, that may be lead, throughout the section. This dark grey phase appears to comprise about 30% of the section; an estimate of volume by the point count method indicates the presence of 24% of this phase. Spectrographic analysis indicates that this bead is made of a copper-high lead-low tin alloy with greater than 5% Pb, 1.2% Sn, 1% Ag, 6% Fe, 0.6% As, 0.8% Sb and 0.2% Zn and traces of other elements as impurities.

The section appears to retain an as-cast structure. There is a small amount of a bright white phase present, probably silver. There are a few very large red inclusions, that appear to be pure copper. There is a small crack that runs the length of the section transversely that may be a result from the cooling of the casting.

The section, when etched with $FeCl_3$, contains an as-cast cored structure with several different phases and inclusions present. The most predominant phase is the dark grey one. There is a distinct red phase that appears to have cooled first and comprises about 40% of the area of the section. There is also a pale phase that cooled after the red one and comprises about 10% of the surface area. There are large spherical inclusions of copper oxide spread throughout the section.

This bead remains as cast and it is made of an unusual alloy. The large amount of lead present would actually be detrimental to the casting by making the object brittle.

517.Sample 27, handle (fig. 741). A partial transverse section of the flange of the handle was sampled. There is no intergranular corrosion present. The section is very regular in shape. There are numerous small spherical inclusions of copper oxide present, and these are slightly elongated.

The section, when etched with $FeCl_3$, contains medium-sized equiaxed grains. There are twins visible but no slip bands. There is a lot of copper oxide present in the form of small spherical inclusions.

The flange has been hammered and annealed as a final shaping of the as-cast handle. It has not been cold-worked after the final anneal. The amount of copper oxide present suggests a poor casting job for anything other than a decorative piece.

Spectrographic analyses indicated the handle as made of pure copper. Analysis conducted at Kennecott Copper indicate this piece has 0.55% As, 0.7% Ni, 0.3% Fe and traces of other elements as impurities, see below. Analysis by the S.A.M. project indicates that the metal is a pure copper with 0.66% As, 0.43% Ni, and 1% Fe with traces of other impurities present, see above, p. 19. A hardness test of this section shows an average hardness of 120 VHN for the flange end.

517.Sample 28, sheet. A partial transverse section of the sheet fragment was taken. In the as-polished section, there are thin outer layers of the common corrosion products. There are numerous small spherical inclusions throughout the section. Some of the inclusions resemble broken "stringers". There is extensive intergranular corrosion present, especially along the edges of the section. This corrosion has outlined small to medium-sized equiaxed grains.

The section, when etched with $FeCl_3$, has medium-sized equiaxed grains visible. The average grain size is 1.3 microns as estimated by point count analysis. There are twins and a few slip bands present. The copper oxide inclusions are primarily spherical with little deformation.

Spectrographic analysis indicates that this piece of sheet metal is made of a copper-medium arsenic-low nickel alloy with 2.6% As, 1% Ni, and traces of other elements as impurities, see below. The sheet has been hammered and annealed into its final shape. It has been cold-worked slightly after the last anneal which would have made the metal harder. The copper-arsenic-nickel metal used is harder than pure copper.

Overall, the technique used to make this sheet is labor intensive given the metal used and the way the metal has been shaped. A hardness test of the sheet metal averages about 125 VHN for the section, reasonably hard metal to use as decorative sheet.

517.Sample 29, knife blade? (fig. 742). A transverse section of the tip was examined. In the polished section, thin outer layers of the common corrosion products are unevenly distributed. The tip of the blade is deformed and very corroded. There are numerous elongated inclusions of copper oxide throughout the section. These inclusions are not elongated in a single direction. There are some "salt and pepper" granular corrosion cavities throughout the section.

The section when etched with $FeCl_3$ contains large equiaxed grains. The average grain size is 3.75 microns as estimated by point count analysis. There are twins visible. The copper oxide inclusions are slightly distorted spherical in almost an eutectic pattern.

The tip of this knife blade has been hammered and annealed from a cast form. It has not been cold-worked after the final anneal and thus not edge-hardened. A hardness test indicates that the section near the tip has an average hardness of 95 VHN; soft metal for a blade tip.

A cross-section from the haft end of the blade was taken. In the as-polished section, there are thick layers of the common corrosion products unevenly distributed. It is very corroded with large "salt and pepper" granular corrosion cavities. There are numerous elongated inclusions throughout the section, and these resemble broken "stringers". There are numerous small white inclusions, probably silver, distributed unevenly throughout the section.

The section when etched with $FeCl_3$, has large equiaxed grains. There are numerous twins visible. The piece has been hammered and annealed from a cast bar. It has not been cold-worked after the final anneal. A hardness test of this section indicates an average hardness of 81 VHN, close to the annealed hardness of the metal used to make the blade. Spectrographic analysis indicates the blade is made of a copper-low arsenic-low nickel alloy with 0.75% As, 1% Ni, and traces of other elements as impurities, see below.

Metallographic analyses: Crucible slag

517.AR, crucible slag. Five small pieces of a grey slag, three of these attached to fragments of crucible. One piece of this slag, $0.7 \times 1.2 \times 2$ cm, was mounted for analysis. It has visible holes caused by escaping gas, copper corrosion products, and lots of iron oxide.

A cross-section of the slag was examined. It is very glassy in appearance and has a few large and many small holes caused by escaping gas. The copper separation in this smelt is very good; there is almost no copper visible in the slag. There are some small covellite pieces in the slag and these do not appear to have been melted. The covellite suggests the use of secondary enriched ores.

The slag appears to be very silicate-rich. There is some fayalite, Fe_3O_4, present but the major component of the silicate is Fe_2O_3. There is some $FeO-SiO_2$ visible. The slag has a low viscosity and good copper separation. The presence of unmelted covellite indicates that the smelting temperature was probably around 1,200-1,400°C. The gas holes and iron silicates present indicate that the copper was reduced under oxidizing conditions, although successfully.

517.BR, crucible slag. Remains of the crucible adhere to the slag. The crucible is made of coarse sand and chaff-tempered ware, and the crucible has melted at the temperature of the smelt. The slag measures $1.6 \times 3 \times 4.5$ cm; it is light grey and contains a lot of spherical drops of copper corrosion product.

In cross-section the slag is glassy and contains numerous small holes made by escaping gas. There are a number of large and small spherical drops of copper present. There is good separation of the copper, but the slag is too viscous for much of the copper to have been recovered. There is some fayalite and fayalite-Fe_3O_4 eutectate present. There is also some Fe_2O_3 present. This slag, like the others examined, contains a lot of silicate versus iron, thus reducing the effectiveness of the copper separation at the temperatures used. The fayalite grains are large and the slag viscous. This slag was probably produced in a smelt of around 1,300°C. The separation of the copper is only fair, probably because there is not enough iron added.

517.ZA, crucible slag. Remains of the crucible adhere to the slag. The crucible is made of coarse sand and chaff-tempered ware, and it has fused with the slag during the smelt. The slag is 0.5 cm in thickness and dark grey. There are several large, 1 cm in diameter, spherical pellets of copper corrosion product visible.

A cross-section of the slag is dark and glassy. There are numerous small holes caused by escaping gas present. There are a number of small spherical drops of copper present through the section. The copper separation is good but the slag was smelted at a high enough temperature to remove the copper. There is not much fayalite visible and no Fe_2O_3. This slag did not have much iron added. The fayalite is present as large grains, which indicates a low temperature for the smelt, maybe 1,200-1,400°C. The low effective temperature is probably a result of not enough iron being added, the low melting point of the crucible, and perhaps the high cost of fuel. Since all of the slags are the result of refining stages, the metallurgical knowledge shown is not particularly impressive.

517.AHR, crucible slag. The fragment, 2.9 × 4.1 × 5.5 cm, has remains of the crucible on one side. It has numerous pellets of copper that has corroded to a green corrosion product. There are numerous small holes caused by escaping gas present. There are also a few areas of brown iron oxide stain visible.

A partial cross-section of this slag was examined. It is dark grey and glossy. There are a few large spherical copper areas. The copper separation seems complete but the smelting was not at a very high temperature, so the copper prills are small. There are some heat-altered rounded grains of covellite present, but the covellite was not melted nor reduced.

The slag contains a lot of silicate, mostly fayalite, Fe_3O_4, and less iron added as a flux or from the copper-iron sulfides than is optimal to reduce the temperature needed for maximum copper separation. The fayalite is present as small grains, which indicates a high temperature for the smelt, probably around 1,400°C, although the covellite is unmelted. The slag is, however, fairly viscous.

517.AID, crucible slag. Remains of the crucible adhere to the slag. The crucible is made of coarse sand and chaff-tempered ware, and the crucible has melted at the temperature of the smelt. The slag measures 1.5 × 5.3 × 6.8 cm; it is dark grey and contains numerous large copper prills and spherical drops, which have corroded to the common corrosion products.

A cross-section of the slag is dark and glassy. It contains little fayalite and no visible iron oxides. There are large spherical and irregularly shaped drops of copper, which have mostly been corroded. There is poor separation of the copper, probably the result of too little iron added as flux. There are numerous holes caused by escaping gas in the section. There are also a lot of copper oxide inclusions present. Overall, this slag is the product of a low-temperature smelt, probably about 1,200°C, and is not an example of good copper separation.

517.AIL, crucible slag. The fragment is 1.5 × 1.8 × 3 cm; it is dark grey and there are numerous small spherical drops of copper corrosion products visible.

A cross-section is dark and glassy. There are numerous holes made by escaping gas. There are numerous small spherical drops of copper trapped in the slag. The separation of copper is good, but the temperature was not high enough and the slag too viscous for good copper recovery. The fayalite grains are large and there is little Fe_2O_3 visible. The slag is quite viscous and there was not enough iron present to reduce the temperature needed to effectively remove the copper. The smelting temperature reached in the crucible was probably not much more that 1,200°C. Given that this is the product of already refined copper, this slag was not produced by a very effective smelt.

Spectrographic analyses

Spectrographic analyses of a number of metal objects were conducted by MMD Research Department of Kennecott Copper Corporation, Salt Lake City. The tests were conducted following the procedures listed by the ASTM. The limits of detection for the elements are: Arsenic > 100 ppm; silver > 0.5 ppm; nickel > 30 ppm; iron > 20 ppm; lead > 20 ppm; zinc > 500 ppm; tin > 50 ppm; and antimony > 100 ppm. Lead, arsenic, tin, iron, nickel, and antimony amounts were read on the densitometer with background corrections made. The standards used were Spex. Ind. CUO in the range 0.1, 0.01, and 0.001. All other elements were estimated visually, including zinc, which could not be read due to heavy background amounts (Heskel 1984 p. 90).

Barbar Identifying Lot	Object Type	%Sn	%Pb	%As	%Sb	%Ag	%Ni	%Bi	%Zn	%Fe
517.A	metal fragment	.005	.002	.008	.01	.01	.04	.001	<.1	.16
517.A	spike	.07	.06	.15	.01	.04	.04	.001	<.1	.4
517.A	rod	.25	.8	.06	.006	.005	<.01	.001	<.1	.15
517.L	sheet	.04	.015	.25	.01	.1	.003	<.001	<.1	1.2
517.L	lump	<.005	<.005	1.5	.005	.03	.004	.001	<.1	.25
517.L or FN	sheet	.021	.085	.17	.007	.1	.3	.005	.1	.09
517.Q	curved rod	.005	.02	.03	.008	.005	<.01	.001	<.1	.15
517.Q	curved rod	.001	.062	.66	?	.005	.05	.001	<.1	.2
517.Q	curved rod	.005	.02	.03	.008	.005	.05	.001	<.1	.2
517.AP	nail	<.005	<.005	1.0	.02	.01	1,5	<.001	.1	.4
517.AY	nail	.10	.006	.12	.013	.06	.34	.003	.1	.09
517.BA	sheet	<.005	.004	.1	.01	.1	.07	.002	<.1	.15
517.BF	curved rod	5	.35	1.1	.05	.08	.8	.001	<.1	.45
517.CB	vessel	.08	.07	1.0	.01	.1	.52	.006	.1	.26
517.CB	vessel	.3	.08	1.5	.07	.1	.55	.005	.1	.35
517.DT	sheet	.06	.065	.2	.015	.1	.06	.002	<.1	.5
517.DX	rod	.005	.02	.25	.01	.1	.07	.002	.1	.10
517.FB	dagger	.4	.14	.35	.012	.01	.1	.003	<.1	.07
517.FD	rod	.6	.8	1.0	.12	.2	.4	.008	<.1	.4
517.FE	socketed spearhead	<.005	.01	.02	.006	.01	.08	.003	.1	.05
517.FN	chisel?	.45	.2	1.5	.15	.2	.45	.004	.1	.7
517.FN	nail	.07	.06	.4	.085	.1	.2	.002	<.1	.4
517.FN	small knife?	.1	.03	.35	.16	.03	.3	.002	<.1	.16
517.YM	flat axe	10	2	.2	6	.1	.21	.007	.2	.17
517.YM	flat axe	<10	.18	.01	?	.027	.18	0	0	.16
517.ZB	sheet	<.005	.006	.95	.001	.01	.004	<.001	<.1	1.2
517.ACL	ingot	.005	.8	.15	.005	.08	.16	.001	<.1	.006
517.AEB	nail	<.005	.055	.17	.007	1.0	.2	.005	.1	.07
517.AGS	socketed spearhead	.042	.27	.7	.2	.1	.15	.15	.1	1.0
517.AGS	socketed spearhead	.2	.015	1.6	.055	.03	.9	.001	<.1	.3
517.AHD	rod	.09	.05	.7	.21	.08	.6	.008	<.1	.2
517.AHI	ingot fragment	.005	2	.3	.25	.6	.1	.008	<.1	.009
517.AHI	fishhook?	.02	.11	2.0	.1	1.0	2.0	.003	<.1	.8
517.AHI	chisel?	.07	.005	.5	.02	.07	.2	.001	<.1	.7
517.AHI	ingot fragment	.005	.005	1.3	.06	.2	.07	.009	<.1	.12
517.AHV	ingot fragment	<.005	<.005	1.0	.004	.05	.25	.003	<.1	.4
517.AIB	rod	1.2	1.1	.12	.03	.08	.04	.005	<5	.06
517.AJH	sheet	.005	.34	.6	.007	.07	.4	.003	<.1	.2
517.AJI	rod	.3	.12	1.0	.02	.1	.2	.003	<.1	.4
517.AJI	shaft-hole adze	<.005	1.2	.1	.02	.1	.08	.005	.1	.12
517.ALB	crescent-shaped axe	1.0	.12	.02	.05	.007	<.1	.07		
517.ALB	crescent-shaped axe	1.0	.004	.12	.02	.01	.05	.007	<.1	.07
517.APG	point of dagger	.05	.07	.5	.045	.6	.7	.01	.1	.4
517.ARV	dagger	2.3	.23	2.0	.1	.2	.8	.01	.1	.6
517.ARZ	bead	1.2	<5	.6	.8	1.0	.02	.08	.2	.6
Sample 27	handle	.05	.1	.55	.3	.08	.7	.004	.1	.3

Barbar Identifying Lot	Object Type	%Sn	%Pb	%As	%Sb	%Ag	%Ni	%Bi	%Zn	%Fe
Sample 28	sheet	.05	.006	2.6	.007	.1	1.0	.01	.1	.12
Sample 29	knife blade?	.02	.3	.75	.03	.1	1,0	,004	.1	.3
681.DA	ring	.65	.5	.25	.01	.1	.002	.003	<5	.46
681.DA	ring	.95	.75	.34	.025	.1	.09	.008	<5	.5
681.EU	nail	.052	.13	.45	.045	.1	.2	.1	.1	.35
681.EU	nail	.013	.15	.32	.16	.1	.2	.09	.1	.7

Appendix 5.
The Well at Umm as-Sujur

At the historically known but now sand-covered spring of Ain Umm as-Sujur Geoffrey Bibby found in 1954 a well-shrine from the period of the Barbar temple (Bibby 1954a). At the end of the excavation it appeared as a well-preserved shaft-stairway leading down to the bottom of a little intact well-chamber. Here follows the full documentation of the discovery.

In the earliest Barbar temple there were found two shaft-stairways in the southwest sector of the temple (plan 1:25-26), which both led down to a spot in the immediate vicinity of the temple-well which had been documented there (plan 3:38). These stairways can thus be considered as parallels to the Umm as-Sujur well. Furthermore, in the Northeast Temple there was a central robber-pit, in which there may well have been a corresponding construction. Thus the Umm as-Sujur well has relevance to these studies. In 1990-96 Japanese excavations uncovered a second shaft-stairway at Umm as-Sujur (Konishi 1996).

Umm as-Sujur is the name of a sand-choked spring east of Diraz, which is said to have been one of Bahrain's most important artesian springs, from which water was led far out across the countryside by way of underground channels. Legend has it, that the spring was destroyed by the caliph Abdul-Malik ibn Marwan (685-705). The name means "Mother of the spring of overflowing waters".

Today the spring has the form of a large hollow, about 70 m long and about 40 m wide, surrounded by banks of sand (cf. Konishi 1996 figs. 2-3). The water-table lies close below the surface, which is covered with vegetation. The well-chamber was found in the southeastern corner of the slope around the hollow (figs. 1-2). Its internal arrangement, and in particular its situation at the edge of a spring where water was directly available, reveals the cult-purpose of the structure. It is a feature which can be likened to the situation at Barbar, where a temple-well and a spring could be localized in the immediate neighbourhood of each other.

In the area bordering the hollow there were in addition found almost 100 large finely-cut limestone blocks, which, however, all lay *ex situ*. Some showed in addition revets and "door-post" holes, showing clearly that they had once formed part of a building. A trial trench in the southwest corner of the hollow, which was not drawn, also found at the foot of the slope four buried blocks of stone, but these too were not *in situ*.

Whether these blocks come from a destroyed wall around the spring or from a building of quite other dimensions than the well, it was nevertheless the well-structure that proved to comprise a connected unity suitable for a systematic investigation. It could be seen on the inner side of the slope to the hollow, in the south-east, where it protruded as a stump of weathered walling from the surrounding sand-bank.

The excavation concentrated on emptying the interior of the structure, whereas the depth of investigation outside was fortuitous. The survey comprised a plan and elevations of two of the walls (see below). The measurements and levelling are accurate, but the co-ordination system used is added to give a frame of reference. The limits of excavation were not measured in. The objective description is not based upon field-notes, but upon the excavator's own published texts concerning the structure and upon information from the pictorial documentation. In addition, the considered account here presented has been sanctioned – and translated – by Bibby.

The structure consists of two portions: an L-shaped staircase-shaft (A) and an adjoining well-chamber (B), all buried in the sand, presumably in a pit dug for the building. Some of the excavation-photographs show a certain stratification in the surrounding sand (fig. 3); it may derive from a filling-up of the building-pit.

The eastwest course of the shaft (A) was preserved to a length of 4 m, but its western end, with the entrance, had been broken off (fig. 4). The north-south course of the shaft (A) was 5 m long, and generally well-preserved (fig. 5). Between the two walls of the shaft a stairway (E) had been laid, about one metre wide, though a little wider at the entrance

Fig. 1. Umm as-Sujur, exposed well-structure, from S. In background, part of the sand-banks around the spring-depression, with scattered limestone blocks and trial trench (1954).

Fig. 2. Umm as-Sujur, exposed well-structure, from NE (1954).

Fig. 3. Umm as-Sujur, well-chamber, from E. Upper portion (1954).

Fig. 4. Umm as-Sujur, east-west stairway-shaft, from W. Between the walls is the uppermost step of the stairway (1954).

Fig. 5. Umm as-Sujur, north-south stairway-shaft, from NW. With view into well-chamber (1954).

Fig. 6. Umm as-Sujur, north-south stairway-shaft, from S. At bottom, 3rd-lowest step and pot-sherds. On 4th-lowest step a fallen roof-block and an animal-figure of stone (1954).

Fig. 7. Umm as-Sujur,
north-south stairway-shaft,
from S (1954).

Fig. 8. Umm as-Sujur,
view into well-chamber,
from N (1954).

Fig. 9. Umm as-Sujur,
north-south stairway-
shaft and well-chamber,
from S (1954).

and a little narrower at the opening to the well-chamber. The steps were about 25 cm high and about ½ m broad. Where the stair turned there was a landing.

The shaft was full of fallen material, among them large tumbled blocks of cut limestone, which had the form of flat roof-slabs. On the fourth step from the bottom was also found a mutilated figure of an animal. The shaft, then, had been roofed, and the architecture had been embellished with sculpture (fig. 6).

All the walling in the shaft (A) was of stones set in plaster. Cut stone can only be seen used for ceiling and steps. The walls (C and D) were coated with plaster on both inner and outer sides, and stood on foundations (C1 and D1), cf. elevations 1

and 2. Two flat pilasters marked the entrance to the landing.

Elevation 1 shows the wall (D), partly length-wise, partly in section at the northern end; it is about 80 cm thick, though thicker where it is carried down deepest. At the top there appeared on the outside a ledge, above the level of which the wall is only ½ m thick. The wall is seen topped by sand (L), a part of the slope which surrounded the hollow. Under the wall sand appears again (K), without this sand being specifically described as subsoil.

Of the roof there still remained a beam-like piece *in situ*, spanning from wall to wall in a position above the lowest step of the stair. Here the wall (D) ended in a vertical line, a corner in towards the well-chamber.

Fig. 10. Umm as-Sujur, view into well-chamber, from N (1954).

Fig. 11. Umm as-Sujur, well-chamber, east wall with niche, from NW (1954).

Fig. 12. Umm as-Sujur, well-head and underlying well-drum, from N (1954).

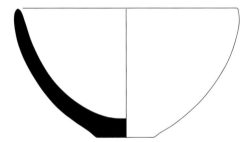

Fig. 13. 1:2.

On the wall-surface (D) the stairway (E) appears as a downward-sloping band of masonry. The upper side of the band shows itself as a sequence of steps, its lower side as a foundation for the stairway. The cleaned-up stairway stood finally freed in its full length (fig. 7). It ended at the top in a landing, where the stair turned in a right-angled corner. At the bottom, just above the stair and below level 3.25, the wall (D) was without a coating of plaster, so that the raw stone wall could be seen. Stones of a length of 15-20 cm were used.

Elevation 2 shows the wall (C), partly lengthwise, partly in cross-section at the eastern end. Here the opposite wall (D) is also shown in cross-section, while between the two walls there appears, in continuation of the stair-band (E), the first step (M) af-

ter the landing. Otherwise the situation is the same as described for the other wall (D). Where the plastering of the wall had flaked off, stones of 20-30 cm could be seen used. The footing of the wall has clearly been sloping, so that the stairway was supported by masonry. The broken outline at the top shows the highest surviving top-edge of the wall.

At the foot of the stair the well-chamber (B) opened up as a specially marked-out little room, just large enough to accommodate the actual well (G) (figs. 8-10). It measured about 1.50 × 1.50 m at the top, and a little over 1.30 × 1.30 m at the bottom. The shaft above the chamber was more than three metres deep and filled with stones, and here too, among the stones, was found an animal sculpture, of the same form as the first. There was also found

Fig. 14. Animal statue, 516.A.

Fig. 15. Animal statues, right 516.A, left 516.B.

Fig. 16. Animal statue, 516.B.

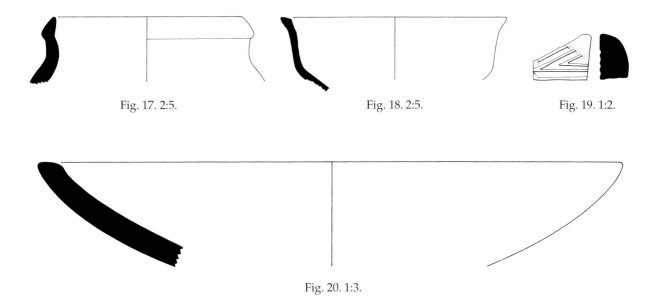

Fig. 17. 2:5.

Fig. 18. 2:5.

Fig. 19. 1:2.

Fig. 20. 1:3.

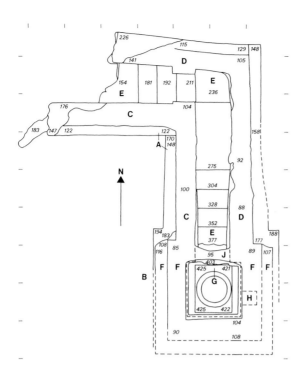

Plan of Umm as-Sujur well. Plan of the structure with appended elevations of two wall courses. Wall course continuation stippled. 1:100.

Plan description:
A. L-shaped shaft for stairs, cf. C-E.
B. Square well chamber.
C. Southwestern wall for stair shaft, of stones in mortar, with plaster rendering on both sides, with external ledge and internal pilaster in front of stair landing.
D. Northeastern wall of stair shaft, as C.
E. Angled stair, of stones in mortar, steps partly of hewn blocks, landing at change of direction.
F. Wall of well chamber, as C, but thicker, with three chamber outlines, one above, one at niche height (cf. H), and one at the bottom (cf. G).
G. Floor of well chamber, with well shaft consisting of well-head and underlying drum, hewn from large stone blocks.
H. Niche in the well chamber's east wall, 36 cm high, 33 cm wide and 40 cm deep.
J. "Roof beam" of stone set in plaster.

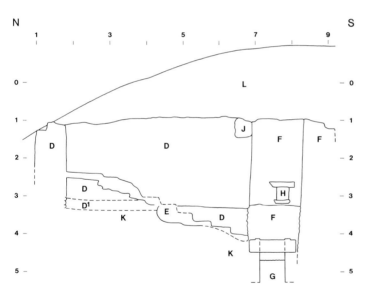

Elevation 1, description:
Inner side of the plan's walls D and F, wall in south-running stairwell and well chamber; description as plan. 1:100. Supplementary:

D1.Foundation wall.
K. Sand without structure: subsoil (?).
L. Sandbanks around spring depression.

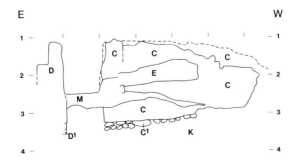

Elevation 2, description:
Inner side of the plan's wall C, wall in west-running stairwell, change of direction between 3 and 4 m, with attached wall D; exposed upper edge of masonry; description as for plan. 1:100. Supplementary:

C1 and D1. Foundation walls.
M. Marked step of incipient south-running stairwell.

a little oblong stone block, hollowed at the top, perhaps an incense burner.

The masonry in the chamber (F) corresponded to that of the shaft, but was thicker. The plaster coating on the walls had also here fallen off at the bottom, below level 3.25. In the east wall there was a deep niche (H) (fig. 11). From this niche the Japanese excavations have uncovered an underground channel c. 10 m towards the southeast (Konishi 1996 p. 89, fig. 4). The drain has an inner height of c. 80 cm and is roofed. At a distance of 5 m from the well a vertical shaft with circular opening leads down to the channel, in analogy with recent *qanat*s, probably a cleaning shaft.

At the bottom of the chamber lay the well (G) (fig. 12). The floor of the chamber consisted of a single large smoothly-cut slab of stone, 1.02 × 1.28 m and 33 cm thick. In this slab was a cut well-hole with a diameter of 72 cm and surrounded by a coping cut in raised relief, 2 cm high and 12 cm wide. The water-table was reached 53 cm below this well-head. Under the base-slab could be seen a 79-cm thick stone block which, like an immense drum, formed the lower portion of the well-shaft. It rested upon sand. The total depth of the well can thus be given as 1.12 m. Elevation 1 shows these circumstances in section.

The floor-slab did not extend quite out to the walls, and in the space between lay potsherds and half an alabaster/calcite bowl, 7 cm tall and 13 cm in diameter (516.D, fig. 13).

The animal-figures confirm the impression of a shrine. They must have been set up as a flanking pair at some point high in the structure, and have not merely served as "guardian" adornment, but perhaps also as a sign of the deity which was here worshipped. A placing high in the structure can be deduced from their position in the excavation. They were not found at the bottom, but relatively high up among the fallen material in the chamber and the stairway-shaft. At the same level as the niche, the chamber was full of fallen building-stones, and among them, by the western wall, lay the first found statue (figs. 14-15, right; 516.A). The second statue (figs. 15, left, and 16; 516.B) stood on the fourth step up from the chamber. Bibby suggested that they originally flanked the entrance to the roofed southgoing "leg" of the structure (Bibby 1954a p. 162). Here there was, on either side, an empty pedestal just large enough to take one of the figures (Bibby 1996 p. 48). The pedestal to the right, when going down the stair, had level 1.04, i.e. 1.07 m above the adjacent step in level 2.11.

The animal-figures are quite small. 516.A is 32 cm long, 21 cm high and 20 cm wide. 516.B is 33 cm long, 24 cm high and 19 cm wide (Lombard & Kervran 1989 no. 52-53. During Caspers 1986 figs. 119-121). They are cut in the local oolitic limestone. Their heads have been removed, making an identification of species difficult, but they are more likely to represent rams than bulls (pers.comm. H.-P. Uerpmann, June 2003).

Most of the pottery found in relation to the structure, i.e. from fill above the stair, between the well-head and the walls and from the well itself, belongs in the Barbar tradition (516.F, H, I, J, K). The following types are represented: Failaka type 1G (fig. 17), Failaka type 3B, Failaka type 29, Failaka type 47, Failaka type 51 (*Failaka 1*), and type B8, type B60 (*Qala'at 1*), a side-sherd with two stamp-impressed ridges (cf. *Qala'at 1*, fig. 237), a wheel-made side-sherd with a plum-red band on yellowish slip and a wheel-made bowl with carinated profile and rim of Failaka type 10A (fig. 18). The wares are late Barbar wares, yellowish-reddish within Failaka ware type C, plus some Failaka type G side-sherds and a single side-sherd in Failaka type H. Besides, a few fragments of Kassite goblets. This pottery finds its best parallels in assemblages found in Areas I and IV 1961, described in chapter 11, p. 242-243 and dated to period IIIa (and b) at Qala'at al-Bahrain.

From within the well a fragment of decorated shell[1] (517.E) (fig. 19) and from fill outside the stair a rim-sherd of a finely-polished stone-vessel should also be mentioned (517.L) (fig. 20).

[1] Identified 1967 by zoologist Dr. H. Schmidt, Bundesforschungsanstalt für Forst- und Holzwirtschaft, Hamburg.

Appendix 6. Phallic Cult-Stones from the Barbar-Temple Period

Three large pillar-shaped limestone columns with a round cross-section and with one end somewhat outcurving have been subjectively interpreted as phallic symbols. One may imagine that such stones have also been erected at the Barbar temple, and one of the stones has also been found in the neighbourhood. A direct connection with the temple is established by two miniature versions from Temple II, the one of lapis-lazuli as an amulet, the other of limestone in a size to fit the hand, cf. the respective groups of finds (figs. 816 and 839).

The three large objects seem designed to fit into a base made for the purpose, in such a way that they would stand vertically as cult-figures. The one end of the pillars is thus irregularly shaped, while the other, outcurving, end is well-carved and must be regarded as the head of the pillar-shaft.

The Barbar-stone was found about 1 km from the temple, north of the village, about 200 m from the sea-shore (fig. 1). The two others are from the neighbourhood of Zallaq, on the west coast of Bahrain.

The Barbar-stone was discovered by P.V. Glob in 1959, after its appearance in a little hill of sand where gravel was being dug. It was excavated by Glob and Mortensen.

A section was laid out across the projecting stone, see below. It records the local placing in the earth, but as the observations gave no cause for more de-

Fig. 1. Phallic cult-stone, found north of Barbar village, re-erected near the temple in an archaeological potsherd-sorting heap (1960).

Fig. 4. Zallaq-stones re-erected during inspection.

tailed excavation it cannot be established whether the stone had originally been erected at that site or had been fortuitously abandoned there. On the other hand, it lay embedded in a layer of sand (3) which contained a number of potsherds from the period of Temple II, while in the layer of sand above it (7) there occurred both Barbar pottery and sherds from later periods, e.g. a glazed rim (cf. *Qala'at 1* figs. 988-89 and 1096).

The actual stone is shown in elevation (fig. 2). It was shaped with parallel oblique strokes about 5 cm long. The elevation shows both the outline and sections through the head and base ends, the former cut flat, and the latter somewhat cut away. The stone is about 2.75 m long, and thereby the largest of the specimens. At the head-end it had a diameter of 42-44 cm. It was brought to the temple and there re-erected, on the western side at some distance from the actual excavation site (fig. 1).

The Zallaq-stones were a surface-discovery, inspected by P.V. Glob and Geoffrey Bibby in 1957. They lay in a date-garden about 3 km north of Zallaq, about 1½ km from the coast, a little to the east of the road between Malikiyah and Zallaq. The inspection could only establish that they lay in the date-garden, where they were said to have been recently dug up. No more detailed investigation was

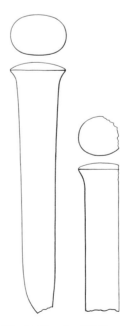

Fig. 3. Sketch of Zallaq-stones. 1:20.

Fig. 2. Elevation of phallic cult-stone found north of Barbar village. 1:20.

made, and there are therefore no datable accompanying finds. The two stones are respectively 132 and 73 cm long and very finely and smoothly carved, the smaller of them, however, being damaged along one side (figs. 3-4).

Section through finding-place of phallic cult-stone, north of Barbar village. 1:20.

Layer description
1. Pure grey-white sand: subsoil.
2. Loose, dark brown sand.
3. Fine, loose yellow-brown sand with scattered stones.
4. Rather dark grey-brown sand with scattered shells.
5. Grey-brown clay with sand and plaster particles.
6. Rather pale yellow sand.
7. As 3.

A. Worked limestone, phallus figure.

Appendix 7.
Bibliography and Abbreviations

AAE: Arabian archaeology & epigraphy. Munksgaard, Copenhagen.

Aaris-Sørensen, K. 1981: A Zoological Analysis of the Osteological Material from the Sacrificial Layer at the Maussolleion at Halikarnassos. In: K. Jeppesen, F. Højlund & K. Aaris-Sørensen: *The Maussolleion at Halikarnassos vol. 1. The Sacrificial Deposit.* JASP XV:I, Højbjerg.

Al-Sindi, Kh. M. 1999: *Dilmun seals.* Ministry of Cabinet Affairs and Information, Bahrain.

Amiet, P. 1986: Susa and the Dilmun Culture. In: *BTAA* p. 262-268.

Andersen, H. 1956: The Building by the Barbar Temple. *Kuml 1956* p. 175-188.

Andersen, H.H. 1986: The Barbar Temple: stratigraphy, architecture and interpretation. In: *BTAA* p. 166-177.

Andersen, S. F. 2001: *An investigation of the pottery from c. 300 BC to c. 600 AD from the Danish excavations at Qala'at al-Bahrain.* MA-thesis (in Danish), University of Aarhus. Unpublished.

Andrae, W. and Lenzen, H. 1933: *Die Partherstadt Assur.* Leipzig.

André-Salvini, B. 1999: "The land where the sun rises…": The Representation of Dilmun in Sumerian Literature. In: *Lombard 1999b (ed.) Bahrain. The Civilisation of the Two Seas.* Institut du Monde Arabe, Paris, p. 42-48.

Aston, B. G. 1994: *Ancient Egyptian Stone vessels. Materials and Forms.* Studien zur Archäologie und Geschichte Altägyptens, Band 5, Heidelberg Orientverlag, Heidelberg.

Azarnoush, M. 1994: *The Sasanian Manor House at Hajiabad, Iran.* Casa Editrice Le Lettere: Florence.

Bangsgaard, P. 2001: Animal Bones from the Barbar Well. In: Karen Frifelt, Islamic Remains in Bahrain. JASP, p. 183-200, Højbjerg.

Barnett, R.D. 1969: New Facts about Musical Instruments from Ur. *Iraq* 31, p. 96-103.

Beyer, D. 1986: Les Sceaux. In: *Calvet & Salles 1986* p. 89-103.

Beyer, D. 1989: The Bahrain Seals. In: *Lombard & Kervran 1989* p. 135-164.

Bibby, T.G. 1954a: The Well of the Bulls. *Kuml 1954* p. 154-163.

Bibby, T.G. 1954b: Five among Bahrain's Hundred Thousand Grave-Mounds. *Kuml 1954* p. 116-141.

Bibby, T.G. 1958a: The hundred-meter section. *Kuml 1957* p. 128-163.

Bibby, T.G. 1958b: The "Ancient Indian Style" Seals from Bahrain. *Antiquity* 32 p. 243-246.

Bibby, T.G. 1965: Arabian Gulf Archaeology. *Kuml 1964* p. 86-111.

Bibby, T.G. 1966: Arabian Gulf Archaeology. *Kuml 1965* p. 133-152.

Bibby, T.G. 1967: Arabian Gulf Archaeology. *Kuml 1966* p. 75-95.

Bibby, T.G. 1986b: "The land of Dilmun is holy…". In: *BTAA* p. 192-194.

Bibby, T.G. 1996: *Looking for Dilmun.* Originally published 1969. Reprinted by Stacey International London.

Black, J. & A. Green 1992: *Gods, Demons and Symbols of Ancient Mesopotamia. An illustrated Dictionary.* The British Museum Press. London.

BTAA = Khalifa & Rice 1986.

Buchanan, B. 1981: *Early Near Eastern Seals in the Yale Babylonian Collection.* Yale University Press. New Haven.

Butz, K. 1983: Zwei kleine Inschriften zur Geschichte Dilmuns. In: *Potts 1983* p. 117-124.

Calvet, Y. 1984: La fouille de l'Age du Bronze (G3). In: *Salles 1984* p. 51-72.

Calvet, Y. & J. Gachet (eds.) 1990: *Failaka. Fouilles Françaises 1986-1988.* Travaux de la Maison de l'Orient 18. Maison de l'Orient. Lyon.

Calvet, Y. & M. Pic 1986: Un nouveau bâtiment de l'Age du Bronze sur le Tell F6. In: *Calvet & Salles 1986* p. 13-87.

Calvet, Y. & J.-F. Salles (eds.) 1986: *Failaka. Fouilles Françaises 1984-1985.* Travaux de la Maison de l'Orient 12. Lyon.

Casal, J.-M. 1961: *Fouilles de Mundigak.* Mémoires de la D.A.F.A., XVII, 2 vols., Klincksieck, Paris.

Casanova, M. 1991: *La vaisselle d'albâtre de Mésopotamie, d'Iran et d'Asie centrale aux III° et II° millénaires av. J.-C.* Editions Recherche sur les Civilisations, Paris.

Ciarla, R. 1981: A Preliminary Analysis of the Manufacture of Alabaster Vessels. In: *H. Härtel (ed.), South Asian Archaeology 1979.* Dietrich Reimer Verlag. Berlin, p. 45-63.

CISI = Corpus of Indus Seals and Inscriptions vols. 1 and 2: *Joshi & Parpola 1987*; *Shah & Parpola 1991.*

Cleyet-Merle, J.-J. & F. Vallet (eds.) 1982: *Archéologie comparée. Catalogue sommaire illustré des collections du musée des antiquités nationales de Saint-Germain-en-Laye. No. 1, Archéologie Comparée. Afrique-Europe occidentale et centrale.* Musée des antiquités nationales de Saint-Germain-en-Laye, R.M.N., Paris.

Collon, D. 1982: *Catalogue of the Western Asiatic Seals in the British Museum. Cylinder Seals II, Akkadian, Post Akkadian, Ur III Periods.* London.

Collon, D. 1986: *Catalogue of the Western Asiatic Seals in the British Museum. Cylinder Seals III, Isin/Larsa and Old Babylonian Periods.* London.

Collon, D. 1990: *First Impressions: Cylinder seals in the Ancient Near East.* British Museum publications. London.

Collon, D. 1996: Mesopotamia and the Indus: the Evidence of the Seals. In: *Reade 1996* p. 209-225.

Contenau, G. & R. Ghirshman 1935: *Fouilles du Tépé Giyan.* Série Archéologique. Paris.

Costa, P. M. & T.J. Wilkinson 1987: The Hinterland of Sohar. *JOS* 9.

Costantini L. & P. Audisio 2001: Plant and insect remains from the Bronze age site of Ra's al-Jinz (RJ-2), Sultanate of Oman. *Paléorient* 26/1, p. 143-156.

Crawford, H. 1991: Seals from the first season's excavations at Saar, Bahrain. *Cambridge Archaeological Journal* 1:2 1991 p. 255-262.

Crawford, H. 1993: London-Bahrain Archaeological Expedition: excavations at Saar 1991. *AAE* 4 p. 1-19.

Crawford, H. 1998: Tokens of esteem. In: *Phillips, C.S., D.T. Potts & S. Searight, Abiel II. Essays presented in honour of Beatrice de Cardi.* Brepols.

Crawford, H. 2001: *Early Dilmun Seals from Saar.* Archaeology International.

Crawford, H., R. Killick & J. Moon (eds.) 1997: *The Dilmun Temple at Saar.* Kegan Paul International.

Crawford, H. & R. Matthews 1997: Seals and Sealings: Fragments of Art and Administration. In: *Crawford, Killick & Moon 1997* p. 47-58.

Curtis, V.S. 1994: More Parthian finds from Elymais. *Iranica Antiqua* XXIX p. 201-214.

Curtis, V.S. 1998: The Parthian costume and headdress. In: J. Wiesehöfer (ed.), *Das Partherreich und seine Zeugnisse.* Stuttgart.

Curtis, V.S. 2000: Parthian culture and costume. In: J.Curtis (ed.), *Mesopotamia and Iran in the Parthian and Sasanian periods.* London p. 23-32, pls. 81-84, I-IV.

Curtis, V.S. 2001: Parthian belts and belt clasps. *Iranica Antiqua* XXXVI p. 299-327.

Curtis, V.S. & S.F. Andersen in prep: A Sasanian site at Barbar, Bahrain. To appear in: D. Kennet (ed.), *Proceedings of the Conference on Current Research in Sasanian Archaeology and History* held at the Centre for Iranian Studies, The Department of Archaeology, and IMEIS (University of Durham), November 3rd & 4th, 2001.

Daems, A., E. Haerinck and K. Rutten 2001: A burial mound at Shakhoura (Bahrain). *AAE* 12:2 p. 173-182.

David, H. 2002: Soft-stone vessels from Umm an-Nar tombs at Hili (UAE): a comparison. *PSAS* 32, p. 175-185.

de Cardi, B. 1972: A Sasanian outpost in northern Oman. *Antiquity* 46, p. 305-10 & plate XLVIa.

de Cardi, B. et al. 1975: Archaeological Survey in Northern Oman 1972. *East and West* (Rome) 25, 1-2, p. 9-75.

Delougaz, P. 1940: *The Temple Oval at Khafajah.* OIP vol. 53, Chicago.

Deshayes, J. 1960: *Les Outils de Bronze, de L'Indus au Danube.* Paris.

Desroches-Noblecourt, C. & J. Vercoutter (eds) 1981: *Un siècle de fouilles françaises en Egypte 1880-1980.* IFAO, Cairo.

Dobney, K. M. & D. Jaques 1994: Preliminary report on the animal bones from Saar. *AAE* 5, p. 106-120.

Doe, B. 1986: The Barbar Temple: the masonry. *BTAA* p. 186-191.

Driesch, Angela von den 1976: *A Guide to the Measurements of Animal Bones from Archaeological Sites.* Peabody Museum Bulletin 1, Cambridge.

Driesch, Angela von den 1994: Hyperostosis in fish. In: W. Van Neer (ed.): *Fish Exploitation in the Past.* Proceedings of the 7th meeting of the ICAZ, p. 37-53.

Durand, E.L. 1880: Extracts from Report on the Islands and Antiquities of Bahrain. *Royal Asiatic Society of Great Britain and Ireland* 12 p. 1-39.

During Caspers, E.C.L. 1971: The Bull's Head from Barbar Temple II, Bahrain: A Contact with Early Dynastic Sumer. *EW* 21 p. 217-224.

During Caspers, E.C.L. 1973a: Sumer and Kulli meet at Dilmun in the Arabian Gulf. *Archiv für Orientforschung* 24 p. 128-132.

During Caspers, E.C.L. 1973b: Dilmun and the Date-Tree. *East and West,* N.S. vol. 23.

During Caspers, E.C.L. 1986: Animal designs and Gulf chronology. *BTAA* p. 286-304.

Eidem, J. & F. Højlund 1993: Trade or Diplomacy? Assyria and Dilmun in the 18th century BC. *World Archaeology* 24/3 p. 441-448.

Eidem, J. & F. Højlund 1997: Assyria and Dilmun revisited. *Proceedings of the Rencontre Assyriologiques. Heidelberger Studien zum Alten Orient,* vol. 6. Heidelberg 1992.

El-Khouli, A. 1978: *Egyptian Stone Vessels. Predynastic Period to Dynasty III. Typology and Analysis,* 3 vols. Philip von Zabern. Mainz/Rhein. Deutsches Archäologishes Institut. Abteilung Kairo.

Erlenmeyer, M.L. & H. Erlenmeyer 1966: Über Beziehungen des Alten Orients zu den frühindischen Stadtkulturen. *Archiv für Orientforschung* 21 p. 21-31.

Fahn A., E. Werker & P. Baas 1986: *Wood Anatomy and Identification of Trees and Shrubs from Israel and Adjacent Regions.* Jerusalem, Israel Academy of Sciences and Humanities.

Fai.cat. = Kjærum, P. 1983: *The Stamp and Cylinder Seals. Plates and Catalogue Descriptions.* Failaka/Dilmun. The Second Millennium Settlements 1:1. JASP.

Franke-Vogt, U. 1991: *Die Glyptik aus Mohenjo-Daro. Uniformität und Variabilität in der Induskultur: Untersuchungen zur Typologie, Ikonographie und räumlichen Verteilung.* Baghdader Forschungen 13.

Frankfort, H. 1955: *Stratified cylinder seals from the Diyala region.* OIP 72.

Frifelt, K. 1975: On Prehistoric Settlement and Chronology of the Oman Peninsula. *East and West* 25:3-4 p. 359-441.

Frifelt, K. 1995: *The Island of Umm an-Nar vol. 2. The third Millennium Settlement.* JASP 26:2.

Frifelt, K. 2001: *Islamic Remains in Bahrain.* JASP vol. 37. Moesgård.

Gadd, C.J. 1932: Seals of ancient Indian style found at Ur. *Proceedings of the British Academy* 18 p. 191-210.

Gale R. 1994: Charcoal from an Early Dilmoun settlement at Saar, Bahrain. *AAE* 5, p. 229-235.

Gardin, J.-C. 1963: *Lashkari Bazar, Une Résidence Royale Ghaznévide. II. Les Trouvailles. Céramiques et Monnaies de Lashkari Bazar et de Bust.* Mémoires de la Délégation Archéologique Française en Afghanistan, 13.

Ghirshman, R. 1962. *Iran parthes et sassanides.* Paris.

Ghirshman, R. 1977: *Terrasses Sacrées de Bard-è Nechandeh et Masjid-I Solaiman,* Mission Délégation archéologique en Iran XLV. Leiden.

Glob, P.V. 1954a: Temples at Barbar. *Kuml 1954* p. 142-153.

Glob, P.V. 1954b: Bahrain – Island of the Hundred Thousand Burial-Mounds. *Kuml 1954* p. 92-105.

Glob, P.V. 1954c: The Ancient Capital of Bahrain. *Kuml 1954* p. 164-169.

Glob, P.V. 1955: The Danish Archaeological Bahrain-Expedition's Second Excavation Campaign. *Kuml 1955* p.

178-193.

Glob, P.V. 1958: Snake sacrifices in Bahrain's ancient capital. *Kuml 1957* p. 114-127.

Glob, P.V. 1959a: Alabaster Vases from the Bahrain Temples. *Kuml 1958* p. 138-145.

Glob, P.V. 1959b: Archaeological Investigations in Four Arab States. *Kuml 1959* p. 233-239.

Glob, P.V. 1960: Danish Archeologists in the Persian Gulf. *Kuml 1960* p. 208-213.

Glob, P.V. 1968: *Al-Bahrain. De danske ekspeditioner til oldtidens Dilmun*. Gyldendal.

Hall, H.R. & C.L. Woolley 1927: *Ur Excavations 1. Al-'Ubaid*.

Hallo, W.W. & B. Buchanan 1965: A "Persian Gulf" Seal on an Old Babylonian Mercantile Agreement. *Assyriological Studies* 16 p. 199-209.

Hannestad, L. 1983: *The Hellenistic Pottery from Failaka*. Ikaros-The Hellenistic Settlements 2:1-2. JASP.

Herrmann, G. 1977: *Naqsh-i Rustam 5 and 8*. Iranische Denkmäler 8/II, Iranische Felsreliefs D. Berlin.

Heskel, D.L. 1984: *Corpus of Metal Objects of the Barbar Temple*. Unpublished report p. 1-135.

Hill, M. & P. Webb n.d.: *An Introduction to the Wildlife of Bahrain*. The Ministry of Information, Government Press, Bahrain.

Horton, M. C. & H.M. Brown & W.A. Oddy 1986: The Mtambwe Hoard. *Azania* 21: p. 115-123.

Højlund, F. 1986: The chronology of City II and III at Qal'at al-Bahrain. In: *BTAA* p. 217-224.

Højlund, F. 1987: *The Bronze Age Pottery*. Failaka/Dilmun. The Second Millennium Settlements 2. JASP.

Højlund, F. 1989: The Formation of the Dilmun State and the Amorite Tribes. *PSAS* 19 p. 45-59.

Højlund, F. 1993: The Ethnic Composition of the Population of Dilmun. *PSAS* 23, 1993 p. 1-7.

Højlund, F. & H.H. Andersen 1994: *Qala'at al-Bahrain vol. 1. The Northern City Wall and the Islamic Fortress*. JASP 30:1. Aarhus. (= *Qala'at 1*).

Højlund, F. & H.H. Andersen 1997: *Qala'at al-Bahrain vol. 2. The Central Monumental Buildings*. JASP 30:2. Aarhus. (= *Qala'at 2*).

Ibrahim, M. 1982: *Excavations of the Arab Expedition at Sar el-Jisr, Bahrain*. Ministry of Information. Bahrain.

IMA 1997: *Yémen au pays de la reine de Saba*. Exposition présentée à l'Institut du monde arabe, Paris.

Jagiella C. & H. Kürschner 1987: *Atlas der Hölzer Saudi Arabiens. Die Holzanatomie der wichtigstens Bäume und Sträucher Arabiens mit einem holzanatomischen Bestimmungsschlüssel*. Wiesbaden, Dr Ludwig Reichert Verlag.

JASP = Jutland Archaeological Society Publications. Moesgaard. Aarhus.

Jidejian, N. 1971: *Byblos Through the Ages*. Beirut: Dar el-Machreq.

JOS = Journal of Oman Studies.

Joshi, J.P. & A. Parpola (eds.) 1987: *Corpus of Indus seals and inscriptions 1. Collections in India*. Annales Academiae Scientiarum Fennicae B239 & Memoirs of the Archaeological Survey of India 86. Suomalainen Tiedeakatemia. Helsinki.

Junghans, S., E. Sangmeister & M. Schröder 1960: *Metallanalysen kupferzeitlicher und frühbronzezeitlicher Bodenfunde aus Europa*. Römisch-germanisches Zentralmuseum.

Kennet, D. 1997: Kush. A Sasanian and Islamic-period archaeological tell in Ras al-Khaimah (U.A.E.). *AAE* 8, p. 284-302.

Kennet, D. 1998: Evidence for 4th/5th-century Sasanian occupation at Khatt, Ras al-Khaimah. In: *Phillips, C.S., D.T. Potts & S. Searight, Abiel II. Essays presented in honour of Beatrice de Cardi*. Brepols.

Kennet, D. 2002a: The Development of Northern Ras al-Khaimah and the 14th century Hormuzi economic boom in the lower Gulf. *PSAS* 32, p. 151-164.

Kennet, D. 2002b: Sasanian pottery in Southern Iran and Eastern Arabia. *Iran* 40, p. 153-162.

Khalifa, H.A. Al & M. Rice (eds.) 1986: *Bahrain through the Ages: the Archaeology*. Kegan Paul International Ltd. London. (= *BTAA*).

Khalifa, Haya Al 1986: The shell seals of Bahrain. In: *BTAA* p. 251-261.

Killick, R.G. et al. 1991: London-Bahrain Archaeological Expedition: 1990 excavations at Saar. *AAE* 2:2 p. 107-137.

Kjærum, P. 1980: Seals of "Dilmun-Type" from Failaka, Kuwait. *PSAS* 10 p. 45-53.

Kjærum, P. 1983: *The Stamp and Cylinder Seals. Plates and Catalogue Descriptions*. Failaka/Dilmun. The Second Millennium Settlements 1:1. JASP.

Kjærum, P. 1986a: The Dilmun seals as evidence of long distance relations in the early second millennium B.C. In: *BTAA* p. 269-277.

Kjærum, P. 1986b: Architecture and Settlement Patterns in 2nd Mill. Failaka. *PSAS* 16 p. 77-88.

Kjærum, P. 1994: Stamp seals, seal-impressions and seal blanks. In: *Højlund and Andersen 1994* p. 319-350.

Kohl, P.L., G. Harbottle & E.V. Sayre 1979: Physical and Chemical Analyses of Soft Stone Vessels from Southwest Asia. *Archaeometry* 21:2 p. 131-151.

Konishi, M.A. 1996: Legendary spring and the stepped wells of 2000 B.C., Bahrain – from the excavations at 'Ain Umm es-Sujur. *Lahore Museum Bulletin* vol. IX, no. 1.

Kroeper, K. & D. Wildung 1994: *Minshat Abu Omar. Ein vor- und frühgeschichtlicher Friedhof im Delta*, vol. I. Philipp von Zabern, Mainz am Rhein.

Kroeper, K. & D. Wildung 2000: *Minshat Abu Omar. Ein vor- und frühgeschichtlicher Friedhof im Delta*, vol. II. Philipp von Zabern, Mainz am Rhein.

Larsen, C.E. 1983: *Life and Land Use on the Bahrain Islands. The Geoarchaeology of an Ancient Society*. Prehistoric Archeology and Ecology Series. University of Chicago Press.

Lecomte, O. 1993: Ed-Dur, les occupations des 3e et 4e s. ap. J.-C.: Contexte des trouvailles et materiel diagnostique. In: Finkbeiner, U., *Materialien zur Archäologie der Seleukiden- und Partherzeit im südlichen Babylonien und im Golfgebiet*. Tübingen, p. 195-218.

Lombard, P. (ed.) 1999a: *Bahrein. La civilisation des deux mers, de Dilmun à Tylos*. Institut du Monde Arabe, Paris.

Lombard, P. (ed.) 1999b: *Bahrain. The Civilisation of the Two Seas, from Dilmun to Tylos*. Institut du Monde Arabe, Paris.

Lombard, P. & M. Kervran (eds.) 1989: *Bahrain National Museum Archaeological Collections. Vol. I*. Ministry of Information. Bahrain.

Mackay, E.J.H. 1929: *The Islands of Bahrein*. British School of Archaeology in Egypt 47.

Mackay, E.J.H. 1938: *Further Excavations at Mohenjo-Daro*. Government of India Press. New Delhi.

Majidzadeh, Y. 2003: *Jiroft. The Earliest Oriental Civilization*, Ministry of Culture and Islamic Guidance, Teheran.

Marshall, J. (ed.) 1931: *Mohenjo-daro and the Indus civilization I-III*. Arthur Probsthain. London.

Mason, R.B. & E.J. Keall 1991: The 'Abbasid glazed wares of Siraf and the Basra connection: petrographic analysis. *Iran* 29, p. 51-66.

Mathiesen, H.E. 1992: *Sculpture in the Parthian Empire*, 2 vols. Aarhus.

McCaslin, D. 1980: *Stone Anchors in Antiquity: Coastal Settlements and Maritime Trade-routes in the Eastern Mediterranean ca. 1600-1050 B.C.* Gothenburg: Studies in Mediterranean Archaeology 61.

Moon, J. 1987: Catalogue of Early Dynastic Pottery. *Abu Salabikh Excavations* vol. 3.

Moon, J. et al. 1995: London-Bahrain Archaeological Expedition excavations at Saar: 1993 season. *AAE* 6 p. 139-156.

Morgan, P. & Leatherby, J. 1987: Excavated ceramics from Sirjan. In: J. Allan & C. Roberts (eds), *Syria and Iran. Three Studies in Medieval Ceramics. Oxford Studies in Islamic Art* 4, p. 23-172.

Mortensen, P. 1956: The Temple Oval at Barbar. *Kuml 1956* p. 189-198.

Mortensen, P. 1971a: On the date of the temple at Barbar in Bahrain. *Kuml 1970* p. 385-398.

Mortensen, P. 1971b: On the Date of the Temple at Barbar in Bahrain. *Artibus Asiae 33:4* p. 299-302.

Mortensen, P. 1986: The Barbar Temple: its chronology and foreign relations reconsidered. In: *BTAA* p. 178-185.

Nashef, Kh. 1986: The Deities of Dilmun. In: *BTAA*, p. 340-66.

Neumann K., W. Schoch, P. Détienne, F.H. Schweingruber 2000: *Woods of the Sahara and the Sahel: an anatomical atlas*. Bern/Stuttgart/Wien: Verlag Paul Haupt.

Nissen, H.J. 1970: Grabung in den quadraten K/L XII in Uruk-Warka. *Baghdader Mitteilungen* vol. 5.

Northedge, A. 1996: Friedrich Sarre's 'Die Keramik von Samarra' in perspective. In: K. Bartl & S. Hauser (eds.), *Continuity and Change in Northern Mesopotamia from the Hellenistic to the Early Islamic Period. BBVO* 17, p. 229-258.

Northedge, A. & D. Kennet 1994: The Samarra horizon. In: Grube, E.J., *Cobalt and Luster, the first centuries of Islamic pottery.* The Nasser D. Khalili collection of Islamic art, vol. 9, p. 21-35.

OIP = Oriental Institute Publications. The Oriental Institute. Chicago

Oppenheim, A.L. 1954: The Seafaring Merchants of Ur. *JAOS* 74 p. 6-17.

Patitucci, S. & G. Uggeri 1984: *Failakah: Insediamenti Medievali Islamici, ricerche e Scavi nel Kuwait.* Rome.

Payne, Sebastian 1973: Kill-off patterns in Sheep and Goats: the mandibles from Asvan Kale. *Anatolian Studies*, vol. XXIII, pp. 281-303.

Pearson, G.W. & M. Stuiver 1993: High-Precision Bidecadal Calibration of the Radiocarbon Time Scale, 500-2500 BC. *Radiocarbon* 35:1.

Pic, M. 1990: Quelques éléments de glyptique. In: *Calvet & Gachet 1990* p. 125-140.

Porada, E. 1971: Remarks on Seals Found in the Gulf States. *Artibus Asiae* 33:4 p. 331-338.

Potts, D.T. (ed.) 1983a: *Dilmun. New Studies in the Archaeology and Early History of Bahrain.* Berliner Beiträge zum Vorderen Orient 2.

Potts, D.T. 1983b: Barbar miscellanies. In: *Potts D.T. 1983a* p. 127-139.

Potts, D.T. 1986: Dilmun's further relations: the Syro-Anatolian evidence from the third and second millennia B.C. In: *BTAA* p. 389-398.

Potts, D.T. 1990: *The Arabian Gulf in Antiquity, vol. I-II.* Clarendon Press. Oxford.

Prange, M. 2001: *5000 Jahre Kupfer im Oman Band II.* Metalla no. 8, Bochum.

PSAS = Proceedings of the Seminar for Arabian Studies.

Qala'at 1 = Højlund & Andersen 1994.

Qala'at 2 = Højlund & Andersen 1997.

Rao, M.S.N. 1970: A bronze mirror handle from the Barbar temple, Bahrain. *Kuml 1969*, p. 218-220.

Rao, S.R. 1963: A "Persian Gulf" Seal from Lothal. *Antiquity* 37 p. 96-99.

Ratnagar, S. 1981: *Encounters. The Westerly Trade of the Harappa Civilization.* Oxford University Press. Delhi.

Reade, J. (ed.) 1996: *The Indian Ocean in Antiquity.* Kegan Paul International. London.

Reade, J. & R. Burleigh 1978: The Ali Cemetery: Old Excavations, Ivory and Radiocarbon Dating. *JOS* 4 p. 75-83.

Reisner, G.A. 1931: Stone vessels found in Crete and Babylonia. *Antiquity* p. 200-212.

Rice, M. 1983: *The Temple Complex at Barbar, Bahrain. A Description and Guide.* Ministry of Information. Bahrain.

Rosenfield, J.M. 1967: *The Dynastic Art of the Kushans.* Los Angeles.

Safar, F. and Mustafa, M.A. 1974: *Hatra. The City of the Sun God.* Baghdad.

Salles, J.-F. (ed.) 1984: *Failaka. Fouilles Françaises 1983.* Travaux de la Maison de l'Orient 9. Lyon.

Sasaki, T. 1995: 1994 Excavations at Jazirat al-Hulayla, Ras al-Khaimah. *Bulletin of Archaeology, The University of Kanazawa* 22, p. 1-74.

Schmid, E. 1972: *Atlas of Animal Bones for Prehistorians, Archaeologists and Quaternary Geologists.* Elsevier Publishing Company, Atlanta.

Shah, S.G.M. & A. Parpola (eds.) 1991: *Corpus of Indus seals and inscriptions 2. Collections in Pakistan.* Annales Acad. Scient. Fennicae B 240 & Memoirs of the Dept. of Archaeology and Museums, Pakistan 5. Suomalainen Tiedeakatemia. Helsinki.

Sjöberg, Å. 1995: *The Sumerian Dictionary of the University of Pennsynvania*, vol. 1:A, part II, s.v. *Abzu*, p. 184-202. Philadelphia.

Srivastava, K.M. 1991: *Madinat Hamat, Burial Mounds 1984-85.* Ministry of Information. Bahrain.

Tengberg M. 2002: Vegetation history and wood exploitation in the Oman peninsula from the Bronze Age to the Classical period. In: Thiébault S. (ed), *Charcoal Analysis. Methodological Approaches, palaeoecologicaal results and wood uses.* Proceedings of the second International Meeting of Anthracology. Paris, September. B.A.R. International Series 1063, p. 151-157.

Tengberg M. 2003: Archaeobotany in the Oman Peninsula and the role of Eastern Arabia in the spread of African Crops. In: Neumann K., A. Butler, S. Kahlheber (eds), *Food, Fuel and Fields. Progress in African Archaeobotany.* 15 Africa Praehistorica. Monographien zur Archäologie und Umwelt Afrikas. Köln: Heinrich-Barth-Institut, p. 229-237.

Tengberg, M., P. Lombard 2002: Environnement et économie végétale à Qal'at al-Bahreïn aux périodes Dilmoun et Tylos. Premiers éléments d'archéobotanique. *Paléorient* 27/1, p. 167-181.

Trever, K.V. and V.G. Lokonin 1987: *Sasanidiskoye serevo (Sasanian Silver).* Moscow.

Uerpmann, M. & H.-P. Uerpmann 1994: Animal bone finds from Excavation 520 at Qala'at al-Bahrain. In: *Højlund & Andersen 1994* p. 417-444.

Van Neer, W. & M. Uerpmann 1994: Fish remains from Excavation 520 at Qala'at al-Bahrain. In: *Højlund and Andersen 1994* p. 445-454.

Uerpmann, M. & H.-P. Uerpmann 1997: Animal bones from Excavation 519 at Qala'at al-Bahrain. In: *Højlund and Andersen 1997* p. 235-264.

Vanden Berghe, L. and Schippmann, K. 1985: *Les relief rupestres d'Elymaïde (Iran) de l'époque parthe*. Gent.

Velde, C. 1998: New Research on the Arabian Peninsula. In: *Phillips, C.S., D.T. Potts & S. Searight, Abiel II. Essays presented in honour of Beatrice de Cardi*. Brepols.

Vine, P. 1993. *Bahrain National Museum*. Bahrain Ministry of Information. Immel Publishing.

Whitcomb, D. S. 1975: The Archaeology of Oman: a preliminary discussion of the Islamic periods. *JOS* 1, p. 123-157.

Whitcomb, D. S. 1978: The archaeology of al-Hasa oasis in the Islamic period. *Atlal* 2, p. 95-113.

Whitcomb, D. S. 1987: Bushire and the Angali Canal. *Mesopotamia* 22, p. 311-336.

Woolley, C.L. 1934: *Ur Excavations 2. The Royal Cemetery*. London and Philadelphia: Trustees of the two Museums.

Woolley, C.L. 1955: *Ur Excavations 4. The Early Periods*. London and Philadelphia: Trustees of the two Museums.

Wright, D. P. 1987: *The Disposal of Impurity, Elimination Rites in the Bible and in Hittite and Mesopotamian Literature*. Society of Biblical Literature Dissertation Series 101. Atlanta.

Wright, H. T. 1992: Early Islam, Oceanic Trade and Town Development on Nzwani: the Comorian Archipelago in the XIth-XVth Centuries AD. *Azania* 27, p. 81-128.

Özguc, N. 1965: *Kültepe Mühür Baskilarinda Anatolo Grubu (The Anatolian Group of Cylinder Seal Impressions from Kültepe)*. Türk Tarih Kurumu Yayinlarindan, V. Seri, no. 22.

Appendix 8. Sections and Plans

Section descriptions

Main Section = sections 1, 2 and 19, cf. fig. 14. Section through temple tell, from surface to subsoil, 1954 and 1957. Key: Temple I hatched, Temple II dotted, Temple III dashed, excavation boundaries dot-and-dashed. 1:100. With supplementary local plan.

Layer description:
1. Sterile sand and gravel with horizontal bands containing plaster.
1a. Stone-robbers' disturbance of the northern terrace wall in Temple III.
1b. Stone-robbers' disturbance of the tell centre.
1c. Stone-robbers' disturbance of the southern terrace walls in Temples II and III.
2. Grey-brown sand with many small stones and plaster rubble.
3. Brown sand.
4. Yellow-brown sand with scattered lumps of clay and plaster.
5. Brown-grey clayey sand with many small stones and lumps of plaster, especially below.
6. As 5, but with fewer stones and less plaster.
7. Yellow-brown clayey sand with scattered small stones.
8. Brown clayey sand, with most clay below and a thin band of bitumen.
9. Dark brown-grey clayey sand with charcoal and burnt bones.
10. Sterile yellow, yellow-brown or yellow-grey sand: subsoil.
11. Brown-grey sand with a little plaster rubble.
12. Brown-grey sand.
13. As 11, but slightly darker.
14. Brown-grey, slightly clayey sand.
15. Pale brown-grey grainy plaster.
16. As 11, locally also with lumps of clay.
17. Brown-grey clayey sand.
18. Yellow-brown very clayey sand.
19. As 11.
20. As 11, but with lumps of clay.
21. Grey-white grainy plaster.
22. Brown-grey, locally clayey sand.
23. Layered grey-black and brown-grey clay, cf. 26-27.
24. Brown-grey sand.
25. Grey-black charcoal-coloured clay with sand.
26. As 25.
27. Brown-grey clay.
28. Layered white-grey and dark brown clay, with locally clayey sand.
29. Grey-brown clayey sand.
30. Yellow-grey clay.
31. Yellow-brown sand with lumps of clay and plaster.
32. Brown-grey sand.
33. Grey-white sand.
34. Yellow sand.
35. As 32.
36. As 33.
37. As 34.
38. Grey-brown clayey sand.
39. Layered grey-brown clay with stones and plaster particles.
40. Grey-white clay with lumps of plaster.
41. Yellow-grey clay.
42. Brown-yellow clayey sand.
43. As 39, but sandier.
44. Yellow-grey sand.
45. Layered brown-grey clay with sand and charcoal.
46. Grey-white plaster.
47. Not described, cf. 48-49.
48. As 45, but with many plaster particles.
49. As 45.
50 - 51. As 46.
52. As 45, but almost powdery.
53. As 45, but sandier.
54. Yellow-brown clay.
55. Dark brown-grey, very clayey sand.
56. As 55, but with plaster rubble.
57. Grey-white sand with abundant large plaster rubble and stones.
58. Grey-white grainy plaster with abundant large plaster rubble and stones.
59. Dark brown-grey sand with plaster particles.
60. Yellow-grey sand.
61. Layered brown-grey sandy clay with charcoal.
62. Brown-grey clay.
63. As 61.
64. As 62.
65. Yellow-grey sand with lumps of plaster and clay.
66. Yellow-grey sand.
67. Brown-grey clay with lumps of plaster, but to the south layered grey-yellow clay and powdery sand.
68. Brown-grey and yellow-grey sand with lumps of clay.
69. Dark brown-grey sand with plaster rubble.
70. Brown-grey clay.
71. Fine white plaster.
72. Grey-white plaster mixed with brown clay.
73. Grey-yellow sand.
74. Yellow-grey sand with lumps of plaster.
75. As 71.
76. Grey-white sand and plaster with abundant plaster rubble and large and small stones.
77. Dark brown-grey sand with plaster rubble and numerous lumps of yellow plaster.
78. Grey-white sand with abundant large plaster rubble.
79. Grey-white sand with abundant small plaster rubble.
80. Brown-grey sand with lumps of plaster.
81. Fine white plaster.

82. Grainy white plaster.
83. Dark brown sand.
84. Clay with lumps of plaster.
85. Yellow sand.
86. Clay containing plaster.
87. Yellow-grey sand with lumps of clay and abundant plaster rubble.
88. Yellow-grey sand with small plaster rubble.
89. Brown-grey, grey-white and yellow-grey sand with abundant plaster rubble.
90. Brown-grey, grey-white and yellow-grey sand with plaster rubble and small stones.
91. Brown-grey clay with plaster.
92. Grey-white clay with many large stones.
93. Brown-grey clay.
94. Yellow-grey sand.
95. Layered yellow-grey and grey-brown sand and clay; the last component assumed from section 20.
96. Layered yellow-grey clay and gravel, and plaster rubble.
97. Grey-white sand with plaster rubble.
98. Yellow-grey clayey sand.
99. Layered dark brown-grey sand in coarse and fine deposits with particles of plaster and charcoal.
100. Layered brown-grey clayey sand.
101. As 98.
102. Yellow-grey sand with plaster rubble and lumps of clay.
103. Brown-grey sand.
104. Grey sand with yellow grainy lumps of plaster.
105. As 81.
106. Brown-grey sand.
107. Dark brown-grey sand.
108. Stones in white-grey plaster.
109. Dark red-yellow coarse sand.
110. Brown-grey sand.
111. Grey, dark powder containing plaster.
112. Dark grey-brown powder containing plaster.
113. Brown-grey gravel.
114. Grey-white grainy plaster with plaster rubble, sandy.
115. Yellow-white lumpy plaster.
116. As 112.
117. Brown-grey stony sand.
118. Brown-grey sand with lumps of clay.
119. Grey sand.
120. Yellow-grey sand with abundant plaster rubble.
121. Grey-white plaster rubble.
122. Yellow-grey sand.
123. Yellow-grey stony sand with clay.
124. Brown-grey and grey sand.
125. Brown sandy clay.
126. Yellow-grey coarse sand with grey strips of sand, yellow lumps of clay and scattered stones and plaster rubble.
127. Brown-grey sand and grey-white powder.
128. Dark brown-black powder.
129. As 128, but sandy.
130. As 128.
131. As 128, but darker.
132. Brown-grey sand with scattered plaster rubble and dark brown-black powder.
133. As 131.
134. Brown-black soil and damp brown-grey sand.
135. Grey-yellow sand.
136. As 124, but with a number of small stones.
137. Brown-grey sand with clay and scattered stones.
138. Grey sand with scattered stones and plaster rubble.
139. Yellow-grey sand.

140. As 139, but rather stony, especially below.
141. As 139, but darker.
142. Disturbance from archaeological sounding-trenches 1954-1955.

A. Masonry consisting of brownish plaster with a little plaster rubble.
B. Masonry consisting of stones set in clay.
C. Masonry consisting of limestone blocks in yellow-grey mortar.
D. Masonry consisting of limestone blocks in mortar.
E. Masonry consisting of limestone blocks in mortar, partly covered by plaster flags.
F. Masonry consisting of stones set in clay.
G. Masonry consisting of stones in mortar.
H. As G.
I. Dressed stone.
J. Pierced stone *in situ*.
K. As F.
L. Masonry consisting of stones in mortar.
M. Limestone block *ex situ*.
N. Masonry consisting of stones in mortar.
O. As N.
P. Masonry consisting of limestone blocks in mortar.

Interpretation section:
A. Sand subsoil.
B. Clay core.
C. Temple Ia, central platform, northern terrace wall.
D. Temple Ia, central platform, southern terrace wall, partially demolished.
E. Temple Ia, central platform, fill.
F. Temple Ia and b, central platform, floor horizon.
G. Temple Ib, central platform, southern terrace wall, partially demolished.
H. Temple Ib, central platform, northern terrace wall under K, estimated.
J. Temple Ib, central platform, extended floor horizon to the north.
K. Temple II, central platform, northern terrace wall, partially demolished.
L. Temple II, central platform, southern terrace wall, robbed.
M. Temple II, central platform, fill.
N. Temple II, central platform, floor horizon.
O. Temple II, central platform, foundation for P.
P. Temple II, central platform, on O, almost completely demolished.
Q. Temple II, central platform, as P, estimated.
R. Temple II, oval platform, northern terrace wall, partially demolished.
S. Temple II, oval platform, approximate northern surface.
T. Temple II, oval platform, southern terrace wall IIa.
U. Temple II, oval platform, frontal stairway of T.
V. Temple II, oval platform, approximate southern surface, behind T.
X. Temple II, oval platform, southern terrace wall IIb, partially demolished.
Y. Temple II, oval platform, approximate southern surface, behind X, estimated.
Z. Temple III, northern terrace wall, partially demolished.
AA. Temple III, southern terrace wall, robbed.
AB. Temple III, platform fill.
AC. Temple III, floor horizon on platform, estimated.
AD-AF. Robbers' excavations.
AG. Tell surface.

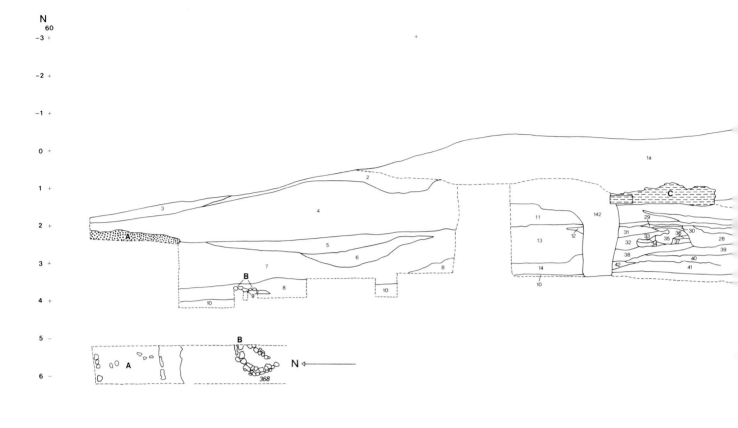

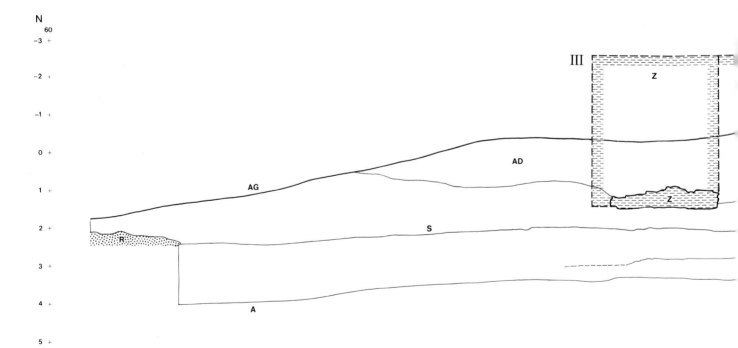

Section 2A, cf. fig. 14. Section through southern part of central platform, from surface to subsoil, 1954. Excavation boundaries dot-and-dashed. 1:100.

Layer description:
1. "Sterile" sand and gravel.
2. As 1.
3. Pale, layered sand.
4. Plaster and stone chips covered by layer of plaster.
5. Stone packing.
6. Gravel.
7. Almost pure sand.
8. "Culture layer".
9. As 7 (?).
10. Clay.
11. Plaster with charred patch on the top surface.
12. Sand subsoil.
13. Stone chips.
14. Dark re-bedded sand.
15. Stone chips.
16. Pale fill.
17. Black "culture layer".
18. Pure stone chips.
19. Almost pure sand.
20. Black "culture layer".
21. Stone and plaster.
22. Pure sand.
23. Sandy plaster or clayey sand (?).

A. Limestone slab: Temple II floor.
B. Worked stone *in situ*: Temple I floor.
C. Masonry consisting of stone and plaster.
D. Limestone block *ex situ*, from Temple II's terrace wall.
E-F. Reverse and obverse of walls, covered by 3-5 cm thick layer of plaster: Temple Ia-b, terrace walls.

Section 4, cf. fig. 14. Section through marginal northeastern part of central platform, from cleared surface to subsoil, 1957. Excavation boundaries dot-and-dashed. 1:100.

Layer description:
1. Sand with plaster rubble and culture remains – sherds, bones and charcoal.
2. Sand with slivers of stone and stone block *ex situ*: soil traces from stone-robbing of the northern terrace wall in Temple II's central platform.
3. Masonry consisting of limestone blocks: foundation wall in Temple II's central platform.
4. As 3, but belonging to Temple II's terrace wall.

5. Fine light grey clay with limestone chips and plaster rubble.
6. Layered "culture layer".
7. As 6.
8. Sand with culture remains.
9. Heavy concentration of limestone chips.
10. Pale grey "culture layer" with charcoal, bedded on head-sized stones.
11. Large stone.
12. Plaster rubble and chips of stone.
13. Blown sand.
14. Sandy "culture layer".
15. As 14, with small stones and some charcoal.
16. Sand.
17. Strip of humus.
18. Transformed greyish material.
19. Pale sterile sand: subsoil.

Section 5, cf. fig. 14. Section through part of central platform, from cleared surface to subsoil, 1955. Excavation boundaries dot-and-dashed. 1:100.

Layer description:
1. Floor slab of worked limestone: Temple II horizon.
2. As 1.
3. Plaster under slabs as 1 and 2.
4. Finely dressed round altar of limestone, partially exposed.
5. "Culture layer": fill in Temple II platform.
6. Rubble layer.
7. Plaster layer: Temple I horizon.
8. Circle of stones in mortar, partially exposed.
9. Plaster under 8.
10. As 6.
11. As 5, but fill in Temple I platform.
12. Pale sand.
13. Brown-grey clay.
14. "Culture layer".
15. Yellow-grey sand.
16. Chips of limestone.
17. Grey clay with offerings: gold band (517.FF) and copper vessel (517.CB) at black triangle.
18. Brown stony sand.
19. Yellow sand.
20. Sand.
21. Sterile sand subsoil.

Note: Layers 12 and 15 contained scattered unburnt bones, charcoal and potsherds. Layer 17 contained the offerings mentioned and a dozen pottery beakers west of the find area, but 10-50 cm in front of the section.

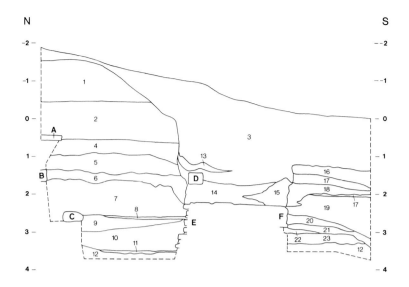

Section 2A

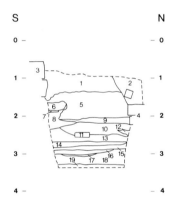

Section 4

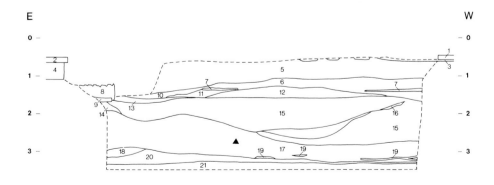

Section 5

Section 7B, fig. 14. Section through marginal west part of central platform, from cleared surface to arbitrary depth, 1954. Excavation boundaries dot-and-dashed. 1:100.

Layer description:
1. Disturbance from western terrace wall in Temple III.
2. Masonry consisting of stone blocks and mortar: western terrace wall of Temple III.
3. Disturbance from western terrace wall in Temple II's central platform.
4. Plaster cast into western margin of Temple II's central platform.
5. Fill layer above Temple II horizon, *in situ*.
6. As 5, but in oval platform.
7. Limestone block with cut holes, flanking stairway, diagonally sectioned.
8. As 7.

Note: The section's levels have been reconstructed during processing.

Section 10, cf. fig. 14. Section through the Eastern Court, from cleared surface to subsoil, 1956. Excavation boundaries dot-and-dashed. 1:100.

Layer description:
1. Grey-yellow stony sand.
2. Yellow-brown stony gravel.
3. As 1.
4. Dark grey-brown powdery material.
5. As 1.
6. Grey-brown sand.
7. Grey sand.
8. Grey sand with yellow lumps of plaster and abundant charcoal.
9. Grey, rather firm powdery material.
10. Grey powdery material.
11. Grey, finely layered sand with many charcoal particles.
12. Grey-black powdery material with scattered charcoal particles, in fine, thin layers, 1 mm to 1 cm thick.
13. White grainy plaster.
14. Grey gravel with particles of plaster and plaster rubble.
15. White, fine-grained plaster, masonry: platform.
16. Yellow-brown, quite firm sand with clay and particles of plaster, appearing as soft plaster: floor.

17. Grey, grainy plaster with many small stones and plaster rubble: floor.
18. Grey stony sand.
19. Grey-yellow stony gravel.
20. Grey-black fine, partly powdery sand.
21. Grey-black sand.
22. Grey-yellow sterile sand: subsoil.
23. Yellow plaster-like sand, cemented together.
24. Grey-yellow stony sand with clay and plaster particles.
25. Grey sand.
26. Grey plaster, masonry: conduit.

A. Masonry consisting of large and small stones in yellowish mass of mortar, rendered on both sides: oval walls.
B. Masonry consisting of cast plaster and flat hewn stones in yellowish mortar: ramp step.
C. Masonry consisting of stones in white mortar: remains of structure inside the court.

Note: Other walling, cf. above, layers 15-17 and 26, etc.

Section 11, cf. fig. 14. Section through ramp to the Eastern Court, from cleared surface to arbitrary depth, 1958. 1:100.

Layer description:
1. Grey-brown plaster with cast-in small stones: floor.
2. Yellow-brown clayey sand with lumps of clay.
3. Brown-black powdery material with particles of plaster and charcoal.
4. Grey-brown sand with abundant plaster rubble and lumps of clay.
5. Grey-white plaster with small stones and plaster rubble: floor.
6. Grey-brown sand with plaster rubble, lumps of clay and large stones.
7. As 5: floor.
8. Yellow-brown sandy clay.
9. Yellow-grey sand, layered with bands of brown-black powdery material.
10. Grey-yellow plaster with small stones and plaster rubble.
11. Masonry consisting of stone in grey-white mortar with a number of small stones, primary below and secondary above

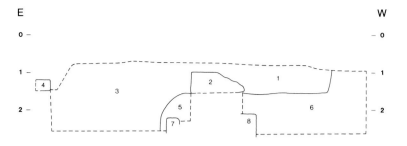

Section 7B

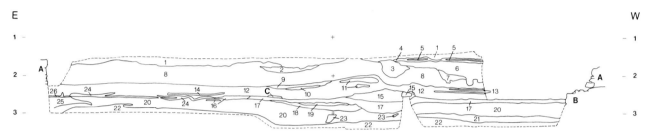

Section 10

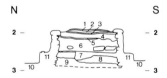

Section 11

Section 12, cf. fig. 14. Section through the temple's eastern foreland, from cleared surface to subsoil, 1956. Excavation boundaries dot-and-dashed. 1:100.

Layer description:
1. Brown powdery sand with small stones.
2. Yellow-brown sand, but below more like 1.
3. Grey grainy plaster with fine-grained plaster rubble.
4. Grey-yellow gravel with abundant plaster rubble and small stones.
5. White plaster with a little large plaster rubble in the layer near A.
6. Yellow-brown gravel and grey-brown and yellow-brown sand containing stone and plaster rubble.
7. Dark grey powder, but locally yellow and locally layered.
8. Grey plaster – in the eastern half of the section grey-black and stony, sometimes powdery.
9. Grey stony gravel with plaster rubble.
10. Slump cavities, the most easterly from a hole dug from layer 18.
11. Pile of stones and plaster rubble in grey-brown gravel.
12. Yellow-brown stony gravel with plaster rubble.
13. Yellow-brown sand with a few plaster particles; grey-brown gravel below.
14. Grey-brown stony gravel; in the right half of the layer many stones and pieces of plaster.
15. Yellow-brown sand, grey-brown below and with plaster particles.
16. Sterile yellow-brown or grey-yellow sand: subsoil.
17. Grey coarse gravel with many stones.
18. Layered yellow-brown and grey-brown sand and gravel, partly stony.
19. Layered grey-brown powder, yellow-brown sand below, and above that grey grainy plaster.
20. Layered yellow-brown powder.
21. Layered black-brown, grey-black or dark grey powder.
22. Grey powder.
23. As 9 and 14, above and below respectively.
24. White gravelly plaster.
25. Grey-black powder.
26. Grey-brown coarse gravel.
27. Layered grey-brown gravel and yellow-brown sand, partially overlain by brown powder.
28. Yellow-brown sand.
29. As 28, but with plaster particles, and locally, grey-brown coarse gravel.
30. Layered grey-brown, grey-black and grey powder.
31. Grey-brown gravel with a number of stones.
32. Grey-brown gravel and sand with a number of stones, in heterogeneous layers.
33. Grey-brown gravel with stones, in heterogeneous layers.
34. Grey gravel.
35. Brown sand.
36. As 35.
37. Yellow sand.

A. Masonry consisting of limestone blocks in mortar, with plaster flags *in situ*.
B. As A, standing on A.
C. As B.
D. As A, but demolished, broken reconstruction line.
E. Masonry consisting of stones in plaster.
F. Masonry consisting of stone in mortar, *in situ*, heavily robbed.
G. Stones from masonry F, *ex situ*.
H. Stone-lined drain in grey-yellow mortar.
I. As H.
J. Stony roadbed.
K. Stone-lined conduit with stone-laid floor.

Interpretation section:
A. Subsoil.
B. Temple Ib, central platform, eastern terrace wall, partially demolished.
C. Temple Ib, pile of stones in front of B.
D. Temple I or II, plaster drain.
E. Temple II, central platform, eastern terrace wall, face partially demolished.
F. Temple II, central platform, wall on E, almost completely demolished.
G. Temple II, central platform, floor horizon.
H. Temple II, plaster drain.
J. Temple II, subterranean conduit.
K. Temple II, stone-set way to ramp.
L. Temple III, eastern terrace wall, robbed.
M. Temple III, stones from L *ex situ*.
N. Temple III, platform, floor horizon estimated.

Key: Sand dotted, plaster black, powdery layers hatched.

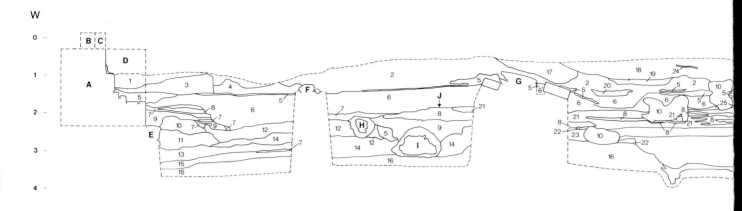

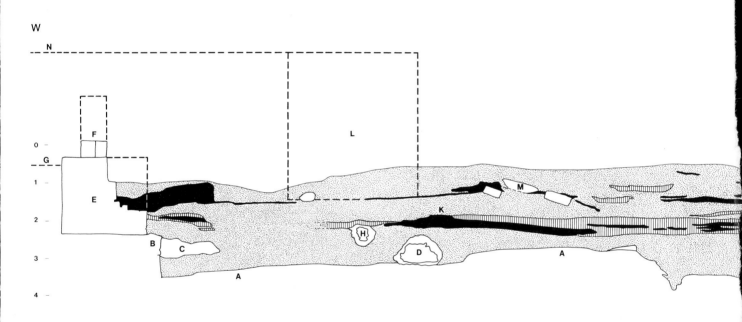

Section 13, cf. fig. 14. Section through the temple's eastern foreland, from cleared surface to subsoil, 1960. Excavation boundaries dot-and-dashed. 1:100.

Layer description
1. Brown-grey clayey sand with many stones and plaster rubble.
2. As 1, but also with scattered lumps of clay, and charcoal and plaster particles.
3. Dark grey charcoal-coloured powder with scattered particles of plaster.
4. As 3, but layered.
5. As 3, but layered and sandy.
6. As 4, locally with a clayey sand layer, 1 m long and 5 cm thick.
7. Grey-brown sandy clay with scattered stones and plaster rubble.
8. As 2.
9. As 3.
10. Beaker sherds in heavy concentration, cf. figs. 277-283, partly bedded in black charcoal-coloured powder.
11. Brown-grey sandy clay with yellow lumps of clay.
12. As 3, but also with small, scattered, yellow lumps of clay.
13. Sterile grey-brown or yellow-brown sand, at the top with wind-blown(?) charcoal fragments: subsoil.
14. Plaster-like sand, natural deposition (?).
15. Brown clayey sand with scattered plaster particles.
16. Yellow-brown, locally clayey sand.
17. Dark grey, locally sandy powder with scattered plaster particles and bits of charcoal, locally concentrated.
18. As 16, but with dark pockets of powder.
19. As 17, but with 2-3 cm thick layers of white grainy plaster.
20. As 17.
21. Dark yellow-grey clayey sand, with lumps of clay and plaster and charcoal particles.
22. As 16, but firmer.
23. As 16.
24. Dark grey, locally sandy powder.
25. Yellow-brown spotted sand.
26. As 17, but with two layers of grey grainy plaster.
27. Grey-brown clayey sand with scattered plaster particles.
28. As 27, but without plaster.
29. As 24.
30. Grey-brown clayey sand.
31. White grainy plaster with plaster rubble.
32. As 30, but less clayey – continuation of 15.
33. As 32, but firmer.
34. Grey grainy plaster with much sand.
35. Brown grainy plaster.
36. As 34.
37. Grey-brown sand with abundant plaster rubble and a few charcoal fragments.
38. As 31.
39. As 37, but without plaster rubble.
40. As 17.
41. As 24, but with many small stones and plaster rubble.
42. Grey-brown grainy plaster with many small stones and a few charcoal particles.
43. Grey-brown fine-grained plaster.
44. Grey-brown sand with lumps of clay.
45. Yellow-brown clayey sand.
46. White grainy plaster.
47. Red-yellow sand.
48. As 24.
49. As 46, but more grainy and locally with thin strips of 24.
50. As 41.
51. Grey-brown clayey sand.
52. As 51, but with a few small stones and plaster particles.
53. As 43.
54. Grey-brown sandy clay with abundant plaster rubble.
55. Brown-grey clayey sand.
56. Red-brown powder with a few small stones.
57. Brown clayey sand.

A. Masonry consisting of limestone blocks, bottom course.
B. Masonry consisting of stone in mortar.
C. Stone-lined drain in clayey plaster.
D. Oval wall in section axis, west end.
E. As D, east end, projected in.
F. Stone-lined conduit.
G. Groundwater table.

Note: Subsoil at -15 m after section 14, between -21 and -31 m after section 10.

Interpretation section:
A. Subsoil.
B. Not used.
C. Temple Ia, central platform, eastern terrace wall, un-der F.
D. Temple Ib, central platform, eastern terrace wall, partially demolished.
E. Temple Ia and b, central platform, floor horizon.
F. Temple II, central platform, eastern terrace wall, partially demolished.
G. Temple II, central platform, floor horizon.
H. Temple II, stone-lined drain, from F.
J. Temple II, oval walled court.
K. Temple II, subterranean conduit.
L. Temple III, eastern terrace wall, robbed.
M. Temple III, platform floor horizon, estimated.

Key: Sand dotted, plaster black, powdery layer hatched.

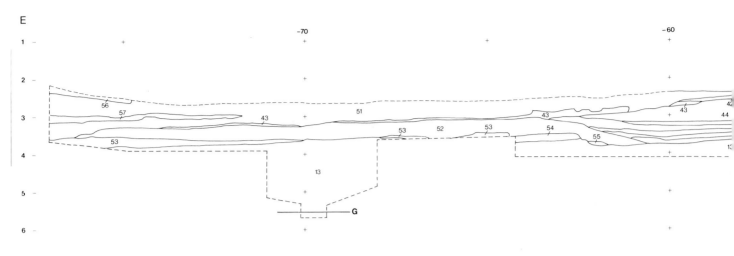

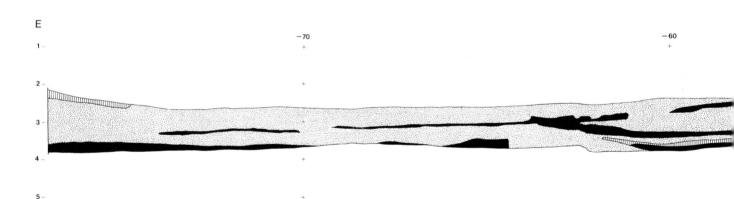

Section 14, cf. fig. 14. Section through the temple's south-eastern foreland, from partly excavated surface to subsoil, 1961. Excavation boundaries dot-and-dashed. 1:100. With supplementary plan, centre baulk unexcavated.

Layer description:
1. Recent disturbances.
2. Grey-brown sand with small stones and lumps of clay, especially below.
3. Black-grey powdery material with very many plaster and charcoal particles, in millimetre-thick horizontal layers: locally also layers of grey-brown clayey sand with large stones or plaster rubble.
4. Dark red-brown ash-like powdery material with plaster particles and scattered plaster rubble.
5. Dark grey clayey, powdery sand with many plaster and charcoal particles, scattered small stones and yellow lumps of clay.
6. Grey clayey sand with large and small stones, plaster rubble and lumps of clay.
7. Brown-grey sand with plaster particles and charcoal.
8. Dark grey powdery material with very many plaster and charcoal particles, and locally lumps of clayey sand.
9. Brown-grey clayey sand with plaster particles and lumps of clay.
10. Yellow-brown sand with lumps of clay and scattered plaster and charcoal particles.
11. Grey-brown clayey sand with lumps of plaster and clay.
12. Grey clayey sand with particles of charcoal and plaster.
13. Sand: subsoil.
14. Approximately as 2.
15. Approximately as 3.
16. Yellow-grey sand with plaster and charcoal particles and many lumps as 3.
17. As 15, but without sand.
18. Not described.
19. Dark brown-grey clayey sand with lumps of yellow clay and particles of plaster and charcoal.
20. Plaster floor.
21. Grey-yellow sandy clay with plaster particles.
22. Dark grey sandy clay with charcoal particles and lumps of plaster.
23. Grey-brown clayey sand with lumps of clay and plaster and particles of plaster and charcoal.
24. Yellow-grey clayey sand with particles of plaster and charcoal.
25. Grey-brown clayey sand with a few particles of plaster.
26. Brown-grey clayey sand with many particles of plaster, plaster rubble and charcoal.
27. Brown-grey clayey sand with many particles of plaster and lumps of clay.
28. As 24.

A. Masonry consisting of stones in grainy mortar: oval wall.
B. Masonry consisting of stones set in clay.
C. As B, block covered in plaster, with plaster floor surfaces departing from its base.
D. As B.
E. As B, south wall plastered, with earth-filled conduit down the middle of the wall.
F. Flat, coarse plaster flag.
G. Stones in clay.
H. Conduit cast in plaster.
I. As B.
J. As B.
K. Sequence of interrupted plaster floors, cf. layer 20.
L. As B.

Section 15, cf. fig. 14. Section through eastern terrace wall of Temple I and II's central platform, from exposed wall corpus to arbitrary depth, 1959. Reconstructed parts in broken line. 1:100.

Layer description:
1. Undressed stones in pale grey-brown mortar and rendered on the outside with the same material: Temple Ib, partially demolished.
2. Dressed limestone blocks in grey-white mortar, and in the upper part in grey-brown mortar: Temple II.
3. As 2, but broken up.
4. Dressed limestone blocks as bottom course of the inner face of a wall upon 2, projected in.
5. As 4, outer side.
6. Original upper edge of masonry 2-3.
7. Local floor level for Temple II, floor of flat limestone blocks.
8. Local floor level for Temple I, plaster floor.

Section 16, cf. fig. 14. Section through eastern terrace wall of central platform of Temples I and II, from exposed corpus to subsoil, 1959. Excavation boundaries dot-and-dashed. 1:100.

Layer description:
1. Masonry consisting of limestone blocks in mortar: Temple II, demolished to bottom course.
2. Masonry consisting of stone in mortar with plastered obverse: Temple Ib.
3. Stone packing in clay.
4. Brown-grey clay.
5. Masonry consisting of stones set in clay: Temple Ia.
6. Brown-grey clayey sand, with gradual transition to sterile sand subsoil below.

Section 17, cf. fig. 14. Section through southeast corner of central platform, from cleared surface to subsoil, 1959. Excavation boundaries dot-and-dashed. 1:100.

Layer description:
1. Dressed limestone block: reverse of Temple II's eastern terrace wall.
2. Grey-white firm sand with lumps of clay and plaster and large and small stones.
3. Grey-white grainy plaster: Temple I floor.
4. As 3.
5. As 3, but grainier.
6. Grey-brown firm sand with plaster.
7. Grey-brown layered sand with small lumps of clay: fill in Temple I platform.
8. Brown-grey clay.
9. Yellow-brown clay.
10. Grey-brown clayey sand, below with local depositions of crystalline gypsum.
11. Brown sand.
12. Yellow-brown sterile sand subsoil.
13. Stone paving.

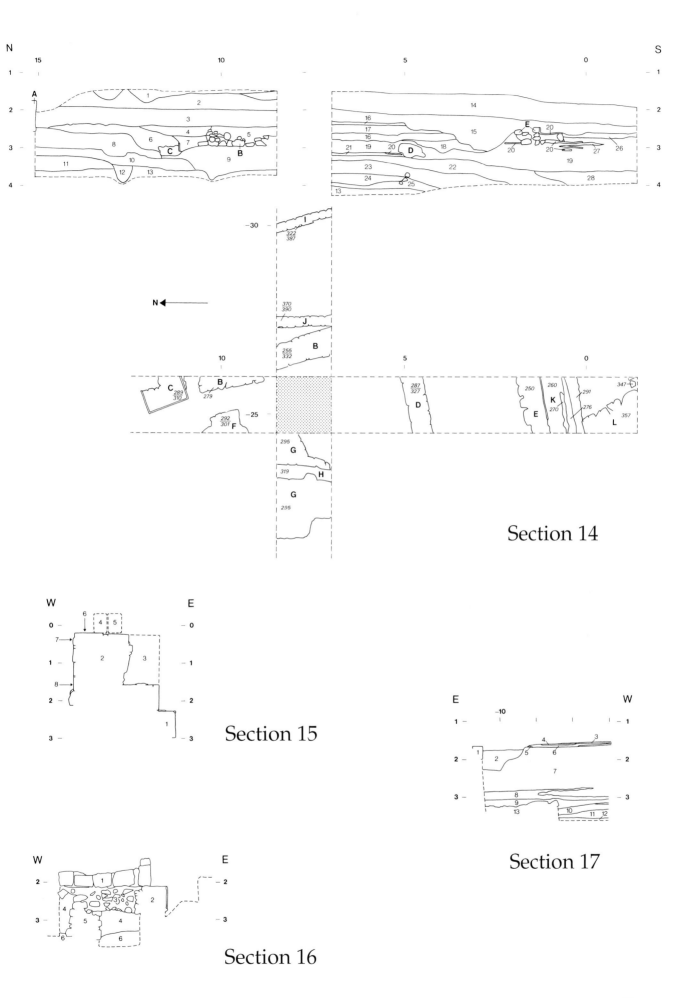

N
15   10   5   0   S

Section 14

Section 15

Section 16

Section 17

Section 18, cf. fig. 14. Section through Temple III's eastern terrace wall, from cleared surface to arbitrary depth, 1960. Excavation boundaries dot-and-dashed. 1:100.

Layer description:
1. Yellow-grey sand with large content of plaster rubble: robbery disturbance.
2. Yellow-grey sand with a number of small stones and plaster rubble.
3. Brown-grey grainy plaster.

A. Stone masonry in pale grey-brown, grainy mortar: Temple III.
B. Limestone block *ex situ*.

Section 20, cf. fig. 14. Section through south part of oval platform, angular, from cleared surface to subsoil, 1957. Excavation boundaries dot-and-dashed. 1:100.

Layer description:
1. Buried cylindrical limestone block.
2. Yellow-grey sand with scattered culture remains.
3. Lumps of yellow plaster in compact layer.
4. Brown-grey sand with many grey-white and yellow lumps of plaster.
5. As 3.
6. Brown-grey sand with thin horizontal strips of clay.
7. Dark grey almost powdery sand with some charcoal.
8. As 7, but paler and coarser.
9. Brown-grey sand with scattered lumps of clay and plaster, with culture remains.
10. As 9, but with more clay.
11. As 10, with horizontal strips of clay.
12. Sand subsoil, projected in from the Main Section.

Section 21, cf. fig. 14. Section through the temple's western foreland, from partially cleared surface to subsoil, 1960. Excavation boundaries dot-and-dashed. 1:100. With supplementary plan.

Layer description:
1. Brown-grey sand with scattered stones and plaster rubble.
2. Brown and brown-grey stony sand with plaster rubble and, locally, strips of grainy plaster.
3. Brown-grey stony sand with lumps of plaster.
4. As 3.
5. Grey-brown sandy clay.
6. Brown-grey, locally clayey sand and local content of stone and plaster rubble.
7. As 3.
8. As 1.
9. As 3.
10. Layered brown-grey and grey clay and sandy clay, with plaster particles below.
11. Brown-grey clayey sand.
12. Yellow-brown sterile sand: subsoil.
13. Brown-grey clayey sand with plaster rubble and lumps of yellow clay.
14. As 1, but with a little clay.
15. Dark grey, locally slightly sandy and charcoal-coloured powder.
16. Yellow-grey clay.
17. Brown-grey clayey sand with scattered lumps of clay.

18. Brown-grey and yellow-brown sand, with a little clay above.
19. Brown, locally slightly sandy clay.
20. Grey-brown sandy clay with scattered stones and lumps of plaster.
21. As 19.
22. Grey-brown clay, locally very sandy and with stones and lumps of plaster.
23. As 20.
24. Grey-brown, partially stony sand.
25. Dark grey-brown clayey sand.

A. Masonry.
B. Floor slabs.
C. Masonry with dressed obverse and adjacent maximum height projected in.
D. Masonry consisting of stones set in clay.
E. Stone pillar of dressed limestone block with moulded base.
F. Stone masonry set in clay.
G. As F and locally built together with it.
H. Drain of stones in clay.
I. Stones.
J. Limestone block: bottom course of Temple III's western terrace wall, projected in.

Section 22, cf. fig. 14. Section through the temple's western foreland, from cleared surface to subsoil, 1957. Excavation boundaries dot-and-dashed. 1:100.

Layer description:
1. Grey-yellow sand with plaster rubble, apparently rebedded after excavation.
2. Slump cavity
3. Grey-yellow and whitish layer of plaster rubble: foot of tell (?).
4. Grey-yellow coarse sand.
5. Grey-yellow sand with scattered stones and lumps of plaster.
6. Grey-yellow sand with abundant plaster rubble.
7. Grey-white plaster.
8. As 5, but very stony.
9. Grey stony sand.
10. Yellow clay.
11. Yellow-grey sand with scattered stones.
12. Yellow-grey clayey sand.
13. Brown-grey sand with lumps of clay.
14. Yellow-grey clay.
15. Yellow-brown sterile sand: subsoil.
16. As 13, but stony and yellow-grey clay below.
17. As 14, but stony.
18. As 5.
19. Grey stony sand.
20. As 13.
21. Grey-black soft plaster or bitumen.
22. As 14.
23. Grey sand with content of grey-yellow sand and yellow grainy plaster.
24. As 13.
25. As 14.
26. Grey sand with scattered stones.
27. As 5, but stony.
28. As 23.
29. Grey-yellow sand and grainy yellow plaster.
30. As 13.

31. As 14.
32. Grey sand.
33. Layered grey clay with a little sand.

A. Walling of stone and grey-white plaster, around four-sided platform in front of oval wall IIb.
B. Grey-white plaster floor on platform as A.
C. As A.
D. Masonry consisting of stone and grey-white plaster: oval wall IIa.
E. Stone-lined drain.
F. As E, stones in grey-white mortar.
G. Limestone block, bottom course of obverse in Temple III's western terrace wall, projected in.
H. Masonry consisting of limestone blocks in mortar: Temple III's western terrace wall.

Section 24, cf. fig.14. Section through pool stairway, from excavated stair corpus to subsoil, 1960. Partially demolished. Excavation boundaries dot-and-dashed. 1:100.

Layer description:
1. Grey plaster rubble layer with limestone, loosely bound together by plaster particles.
2. Grey-brown clayey sand.
3. Yellow, coarse, grainy plaster.
4. Yellow-grey clay with occasional red-yellow patches.
5. Brown-grey sandy clay.
6. Yellow-brown sterile sand: subsoil.

A. Dressed limestone block with square holes in the surface.
B. As A.
C. Finely dressed block of dense white limestone: stair string.
D. As C.
E. Roughly dressed stone.
F. As E.

Section 25, cf. fig. 14. Section through pool, from cleared surface to arbitrary depth, but to subsoil in the north, 1959. Excavation boundaries dot-and-dashed. 1:100.

Layer description:
1. Grey-brown clayey sand with many small stones and lumps of plaster and clay.
2. Grey- and yellow-brown sand with scattered lumps of clay.
3. Grey- and yellow-brown sand with very thin horizontal strips of clay.
4. As 2.
5. Brown sandy clay with many stones and plaster rubble above towards the south: from wall B.
6. White plaster.
7. Yellow-brown fine, clean sand.
8. Grey-brown clay with stones and plaster rubble.
9. As 7, but with masses of stone rubble, also large.
10. Large stone in 9.
11. As 10.
12. As 7.
13. Brown clay with a few small stones and plaster rubble.
14. As 13, but grey-brown.

15. As 14, but with greater content of small stones.
16. Grey-brown clayey sand with lumps of clay and scattered plaster particles.
17. Grey-brown fine sand.
18. As 17.
19. As 16, but with a greater number of small stones.
20. Grey-yellow sterile sand: subsoil.

A. Masonry consisting of stones set in clay: south wall of pool.
B. Masonry consisting of stones and dressed limestone blocks in clay and plaster: south wall of pool.
C. Masonry consisting of large finely-dressed limestone blocks: south wall of pool.
D. As C.
E. Dressed limestone block in side wall of pool stairway.
F. Steps of pool stairway, finely cut from white limestone, cf. section 33, step 6.
G. As F, cf. section 33, step 7.
H. Masonry consisting of large, finely dressed limestone blocks in white mortar.
I. Masonry consisting of large and small stones, set in clay, bottom course.

Section 26A, cf. fig. 14. Section through southwestern margin of the tell, from cleared surface to subsoil, locally only to arbitrary depth, 1957. Excavation boundaries dot-and-dashed. 1:100.

Layer description:
1. Yellow-grey layered sand with very large amounts of plaster rubble: robbers' disturbance.
2. Grey-white plaster.
3. Layered brown and yellow-grey clay and clayey sand with numerous plaster rubble, especially towards the top.
4. Grey-black clay with much charcoal and concentrations of potsherds.
5. Brown-grey clay, dark above, pale below; more sandy above than below, above with scatter of plaster rubble. On the surface a 2-5 cm thick strip of grey-black clay with charcoal, extending in under A.
6. Grey-brown sandy clay.
7. Yellow-grey sterile sand: subsoil.
8. Brown-grey sand with lumps of clay and plaster.
9. Grey-white plaster, closely adhering: floor.
10. Fine pale brown-grey sand, drift sand (?).
11. As 3, but with fewer plaster rubble.
12. Brown-grey layered sand, locally with clay lumps in bands: excavation.
13. Pale grey-brown sand with lumps of plaster and clay.
14. Pale grey-brown stony sand.

A. Masonry consisting of stones set in clay: Temple Ib, foundation for southern terrace wall.
B. Stone stairway, projected in from nearby position.
C. Masonry consisting of stones and plaster, set in white plaster; outer surfaces rendered in pale yellow-brown plaster: Temple III, southern terrace wall near well.
D. Masonry consisting of stones set in white plaster, obverse with facet and above level 4.15 rendered in white plaster, which is poorly preserved below this level.

Section 26B, cf. fig. 14. Section through temple well, from cleared surface to arbitrary depth, 1957. Excavation boundaries dot-and-dashed. 1:100. With situation plan.

Situation plan:
1. Fragment of Temple III's terrace wall.
2. Temple II, oval wall IIa.
3. Facet on 2.
4. Well drum, Temple IIb, cf. section (C–H).

Layer description:
1. Pale grey-brown sand with a number of stones and plaster rubble.
2. As 1, but more stony.
3. Stone and rubble layer in pale grey-brown sand, cemented together.
4. As 1, but with only a few stones and little plaster rubble.
5. Pale grey-brown sand with scattered lumps of plaster and clay.
6. Grey-brown to brown sand, dug up from 8 (?).
7. Pale grey-yellow fine sand devoid of culture remains, drift sand (?).
8. As 6, but layered in alternating brown and grey-brown horizons, of which the brown contain some charcoal and culture remains while the grey-brown are sterile.

A. Masonry consisting of stones and plaster rubble, set in white mortar: Temple III well.
B. As A.
C. Well drums cast in stones and mortar: Temple IIb, opposite side = D1–E1.
D–H. Well shaft, with inner sides of well drums projected in; D fragmented.
D1–H1. Cast well drums as C, H from stated measurements.

Section 26C, cf. fig. 14. Section through southwestern margin of the tell, from cleared surface to arbitrary depth, 1957. Excavation boundaries dot-and-dashed. 1:100.

Layer description:
1. Grey-brown sand with many stones and plaster rubble.
2. Grey-brown sand with lumps of plaster and clay, increasing in number below.
3. Yellow grainy, rather loose plaster.
4. Grey-brown sand with scattered plaster rubble.
5. Grey-white plaster rubble.
6. As 2, but with fewer lumps.
7. Grey-brown sand with some plaster rubble and a marked content of culture remains.
8. Grey-brown and brown sand, dug up from 10 (?).
9. Grey-yellow fine sand without culture remains: drift sand (?).

10. Grey-brown and brown sand in alternating horizontal bands, the brown with culture remains, the grey-brown without.

A. Masonry consisting of stones and plaster rubble, set in white mortar: Temple III's southern terrace wall.
B. Masonry consisting of stones set in white mortar, obverse with facet and above level 4.15 rendered in white plaster: oval wall IIa.
C. As A, by temple well.

Section 27A, cf. fig. 14. Section through southwestern margin of the tell, from cleared surface to subsoil, 1957. Excavation boundaries dot-and-dashed. 1:100.

Layer description
1. Brown-grey sand with lumps of clay and plaster rubble.
2. Dark yellow-grey sand with pockets of brown-grey and grey-black sand.
3. As 2, but paler and with lumps of brown-grey and grey-black sand in horizontal bands.
4. Brown-grey sand with small plaster rubble, sometimes scattered, sometimes obliquely bedded and following the top of the layer.
5. Brown-grey slightly clayey sand with a little plaster rubble.
6. Grey-white plaster rubble.
7. Pale brown-grey sand with firm patches of sand, drift sand (?).
8. Brown-grey slightly clayey sand, deposited in alternating dark and pale bands, cf. section 27C (21).
9. Yellow-grey sand with a little plaster rubble.
10. Yellow-grey sand with some stones at the top and only a few culture remains: incipient subsoil (?).
11. As 1.
12. Plaster rubble in sand.
13. Fine brown-grey sand with a little charcoal.
14. Yellow-grey clay with gravel and sand and a few plaster rubble.
15. Yellow-grey fine sand with scattered pockets of coarse sand and small stones: subsoil (?).
16. Yellow-grey sand with a few small stones, small lumps of clay and plaster particles.
17. As 14, but with more clay.

A. Masonry consisting of stones set in grey-white mortar, obverse rendered in white plaster, stopping below at level 4.40: oval wall IIa.
B. Dressed limestone blocks: demolished temple IIb masonry.
C. Masonry consisting of large stones and plaster rubble, set in clay, sand and plaster.
D. Masonry: foundation for the string-blocks of the pool steps.

Section 27C, fig. 14. Section through southwestern margin of the tell, from cleared surface to arbitrary depth, 1957. Excavation boundaries dot-and-dashed. 1:100.

Layer description:
1. Plaster rubble in sand.
2. Yellow-grey clay with a few plaster rubble.
3. Brown-grey sand.
4. Yellow-grey clay with gravel or sand.
5. Brown-grey sand with lumps of clay and considerable plaster rubble.
6. Yellow-grey clay with abundant plaster rubble.
7. Brown-grey layered sand with clay and plaster, obliquely bedded following the top of the layer, but with a greater content of clay below than above.
8. Unexcavated stair core, subsoil level to the north marked with an arrow.
9. As 5, but with less plaster rubble.
10. Grey-white plaster rubble; depression at the southern end of the layer mixed with 9.
11. Yellow-grey sand.
12. Brown-grey firm sand with plaster rubble.
13. Plaster.
14. Yellow-grey sandy clay with scattered plaster rubble.
15. Brown-grey sand with a few lumps of clay.
16. Brown-grey sand with scattered plaster rubble.
17. As 16.
18. Brown-grey sand with bands of clay and abundant plaster rubble.
19. Yellow-grey sand with lumps of brown-grey and grey-black sand in horizontal bands.
20. Pale brown-grey sand with firm accumulations of sand, drift sand (?).
21. Brown-grey, slightly clayey sand, deposited in alternating light and dark bands.

A. Masonry consisting of stones and plaster rubble, in grey-white mortar: western terrace wall, Temple III.
B. Dressed stone: foundation for string of the pool stairway.
C. Masonry consisting of stones set in grey-white mortar, obverse rendered in white plaster; the section cuts two steps of lateral stairs built on, 12th and 13th step from the top: oval wall IIa.
D. Stone stair set in clay and plaster: Temple Ia.
E. Stones: foundation for F.
F. Slab on edge, projected in from nearby position.

Section 27D, cf. fig. 14. Section through part of pool stairs, from cleared surface to subsoil, 1957. Excavation boundaries dot-and-dashed. 1:100.

Layer description:
1. Plaster rubble and cemented sand.
2. Brown-grey sand with lumps of clay and plaster rubble.
3. Brown-grey sand.
4. Yellow-grey clay with gravel, scattered plaster rubble and large stones.
5. Yellow-grey sterile sand with scattered pockets of coarse sand and small stones: subsoil.
6. As 1.
7. Fine yellow-grey sand resembling a drift layer.
8. As 3.
9. As 4.

A. Dressed limestone block, portal step in the pool stairs, reconstruction of continued course in broken line.
B. Dressed limestone block, *ex situ*, from obverse of Temple III's western terrace wall.

Section 28, cf. fig. 14. Section through southwest foreland of the temple, from surface to arbitrary depth, 1961. Excavation boundaries dot-and-dashed. 1:100. With supplementary surface plan.

Layer description:
1. Grey-brown sand with scattered bits of plaster.
2. Grey clayey sand with scattered lumps of clay and plaster particles.
3. Grey clay with many stones.
4. Grey-brown clay.
5. Yellow to yellow-brown sand with plaster rubble.
6. Grey-brown clayey sand with plaster particles and charcoal.
7. Grey sand with plaster particles.
8. Brown-grey powdery sandy clay with particles of plaster and charcoal.
9. Brown-grey sandy clay with particles of plaster and charcoal.
10. As 9, but stony.
11. Irregular pile of stones in clayey sand.
12. Yellow to brown-grey sand with scattered small stones.
13. Brown-grey sand with plaster particles.
14. Yellow-brown clayey sand.
15. Grey clayey sand with plaster particles.
16. Brown-grey clayey sand.

A. Plastered inner side of wall, perpendicular to B.
B. Masonry consisting of stones set in clay; on the eastern inner aspect of the wall remains of darkened plaster rendering.
C. Large stones in a row, without mortar: wall foundation (?).
D. Masonry consisting of stones set in clay, with plaster rendering on the western inner aspect of the wall.
E. Clayey plaster with embedded small stones: floor, hole stippled.

Section 29, cf. fig. 14. Section through southwestern foreland of the temple, from surface to subsoil, 1961. Excavation boundaries dot-and-dashed. 1:100. With supplementary plans.

Layer description:
1. Grey-brown clayey sand with plaster particles.
2. Grey-brown sand with abundant stones and plaster rubble, dark brown below, perhaps slightly clayey and powdery.
3. Layer of stones in clayey sand with abundant plaster rubble.
4. Masonry consisting of stones set in clayey sand.
5. Yellow-brown sand.
6. Masonry consisting of stones set in clay with underlying accumulation of stones.
7. Brown clayey sand, locally with concentrations of stones and plaster rubble.
8. Block of white plaster with edging wall to the right.

9. Grey-brown powdery clayey sand with plaster particles.
10. White plaster.
11. Grey sand with dense cementation of pieces of plaster and stone.
12. Masonry consisting of stones set in clay, with remains of plaster rendering on the east side.
13. Yellow-brown sand with scattered lumps of clay.
14. Dressed limestone block.
15. Not described.
16. Heap of stones.
17. Grey-brown clayey sand with charcoal and plaster particles.
18. Grey-brown clayey sand with lumps of plaster and clay and many bones and shells.
19. Masonry consisting of stones set in sandy clay, projected in.
20. Grey-brown clayey sand with many plaster fragments and bones.
21. Yellow or grey-brown sand.
22. Grey-brown lumpy clay with small stones.
23. As 22, but slightly darker.
24. Grey-yellow plastic clay with small shells.
25. Grey-brown clayey sand with plaster particles and bits of bone.
26. Grey-yellow, slightly clayey fine sand with shells, water-deposited (?): subsoil.
27. Stones without mortar: wall foundation (?), projected in.

Note: Groundwater appeared at the deepest part of the excavation.

Section 30, cf. fig. 14. Section through northern part of the temple foreland, from partially excavated surface to subsoil, 1960. Excavation boundaries dot-and-dashed. 1:100. With supplementary plan.

Layer description:
1. Yellow-brown sand with stones and pieces of plaster.
2. As 1.
3. Grey-brown sand with scattered lumps of clay and plaster particles.
4. Grey-brown clayey sand with scattered pieces of plaster and charcoal particles.
5. Brown clayey sand.
6. Yellow-brown sand: subsoil.
7. Grey-brown clay with scattered pieces of plaster and charcoal particles.
8. Grey-brown clayey sand with scattered lumps of clay.
9. Grey-brown sandy clay with scattered plaster particles.
10. Brown-grey clayey sand.

A. Stone masonry with plaster core: oval wall IIb.
B. Masonry consisting of stones in clay: Temple I's oval wall (?).

Section 31, cf. fig. 14. Section through northern foreland of the temple, from partially cleared surface to subsoil and arbitrary depth, 1960. Excavation boundaries dot-and-dashed. 1:100. With supplementary plan.

Layer description:
1. Grey-brown sand with a few scattered pieces of plaster and plaster particles.
2. As 1, but with more plaster particles.
3. Grey-brown stony clayey sand,
4. Grey-brown sand with scattered small lumps of clay and plaster particles.
5. Grey-brown clayey sand with scattered lumps of clay and plaster.
6. Yellow-brown fine sterile sand: subsoil.
7. Grey-brown sand with abundant small plaster rubble.
8. Rather dark grey clayey sand, fine and almost powdery, with charcoal and grey-white ash-like lumps in addition to scattered lumps of plaster and clay.
9. As 8, but layered in 2-3 cm thick layers that alternate with white plaster-like mass containing charcoal and bones.
10. Rather dark grey clayey sand, fine and with a great quantity of charcoal.
11. As 5, but darker and with a large content of charcoal.
12. Grey-brown sand with many stones and lumps of plaster and clay.

A-C. Masonry consisting of stones set in clay.

Section 33. Reconstruction section through pool and pool stairway. Elements *in situ* shown in unbroken line. 1:100. 1-30. Pool stair.

A. Central platform.
B. Oval platform.
C. West wall of pool.
D. North wall of pool.
E. Channel opening in D.
F. Rabbet in D.
G. Normal water level,
H. West chamber in pool.
I. East chamber in pool.
J. Bottom of H.
K. East wall of H.
L. Bottom of I.
M. North wall of I.
N. Ledge in east side of I.
O. Mark (?).
P. Portal foundation.
Q. Stair string.
R. Flanking stone blocks with cut holes.

Section 34, cf. plan 10. Section through tell of Northeast Temple, from surface to subsoil. Excavation boundaries dot-and-dashed. 1:100. Layers 1-11 excavated in 1961 projected in on the section axis from 1956.

Layer description:
1. Sterile sand: subsoil.
2. Slightly clayey sand.
3-4. Sand.
5. Dark powdery material.
6. Sand.
7. Clayey sand.
8. As 7.
9. Clayey stony sand.
10. Clayey sand with dressed limestone blocks *ex situ.*
11. Sand.
12. Gravelly sand with a number of small stones.
13. As 12, but with fewer stones.
14. Gravelly sand.
15. Gravelly sand with a few small stones, the upper part cemented together and covered by a c. 10 cm thick layer of crushed stony plaster.
16. Gravel, slightly stony, with horizons of crushed plaster and covered by a layer of plaster.
17. Gravelly sand, slightly stony, the upper part strongly cohesive.
18. Gravelly sand, slightly stony, deposited in oblique layers, sloping from outside and in towards the middle of the tell, the upper part strongly cohesive.
19. Sandy gravel.
20. As 17.
21. As 20.
22. Gravelly sand, covered by a thin layer of plaster.
23. As 22.
24. Gravelly sand.
25. As 24, but strongly cohesive.

A. Foundation layer of stones and plaster, breached by excavation D, edged with stones.
B. Robbers' excavation for inner wall on A, foundation wall. Filled with gravel and sand, layered above as after drift. The western disturbance below very stony, the eastern somewhat less so.
C. Stone-robbers' excavation of the outer wall on A, terrace wall. Filled with extremely stony gravel. The western disturbance with wall fragment *in situ* (C1) and large wall stud (E), the eastern also filled with large dressed limestone blocks and cohesive pieces of wall consisting of stones in mortar.
C1. Back of outer wall *in situ.*
D. Stone robbers' excavation in the centre of the tell, longitudinal section, breaching A, filled with gravel and very stony.
E. Masonry consisting of stone and plaster, tumbled stud, covered by crushed plaster.
F. Robbers' excavation in eastern tell foot, presumably for terrace wall of lower platform, filled by layers 5-7.
G. Plaster layer on rubble foundation.

Interpretation section:
A. Foundation layer of upper platform.
B. Foundation wall for building on upper platform, with stone-robbers' disturbance.
C. Terrace wall around upper platform, with stone-robbers' disturbance.
D. Central structure in double terrace, with stone-robbers' disturbance.
E. Tumbled wall stud.
F. Terrace wall on lower platform, with stone-robbers' disturbance.
G. Layer of plaster on lower platform.
H. Subsoil surface.
I. Fill in lower platform.
J. Fill in upper platform.
K. Floor horizon for lower platform.
L. Floor horizon for upper platform.
M. Tell surface.

Section 35, cf. plan 10. Section through tell of Northeast Temple, from surface to foundation layer, but in the centre down to subsoil. Excavation boundaries dot-and-dashed. 1:100. Layers 1-5 excavated in 1961 projected in on section axis from 1956.

Layer description:
1. Sterile sand: subsoil (?).
2. Clayey sand.
3. Clayey sand with many stones: demolition layer (?).
4. Clayey sand.
5. Sand with plaster rubble.
6. Gravelly sand with stones, strongly cohesive above.
7. Gravelly sand, sand below, with stones.
8. Crushed plaster.
9. Gravelly sand.
10. Gravel with very many stones, local pit.
11. Gravelly sand, covered by thin layer of plaster.
12. Sand.
13. Gravelly sand with a few stones, strongly cohesive above.
14. As 13.
15. Sandy gravel.
16. Sandy gravel with a few stones.
17. Sand covered by thin layer of plaster.
18. Gravelly sand with a few stones and small layers of powdery plaster-like mass.
19. Sand covered by thin layer of plaster.

A. As section 34(A), but broken up at both ends, breached for D.
B. As section 34(B), southern disturbance slightly stony below, northern devoid of stones.
C. As section 34(C); northern soil change contained at the far end a heap of shells.
D. As section 34(D), cross-section. Under the A horizon filled up completely with stones and wall fragments and four finely worked limestone blocks, all in an irregular heap.
E. Small excavation in the south, filled with very stony gravel.
F. Masonry consisting of stone and plaster, isolated stud (?).

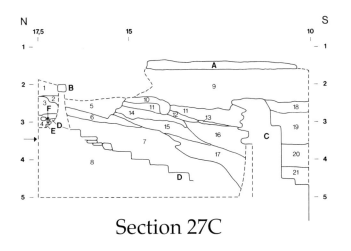

Section 27C

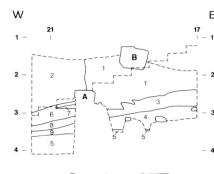

Section 27D

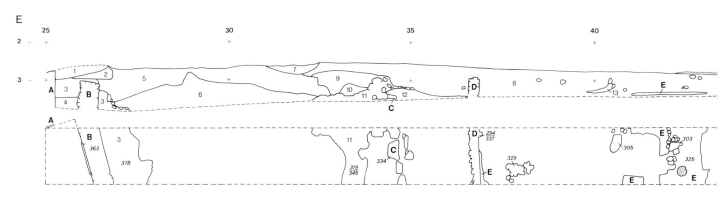

Section 28

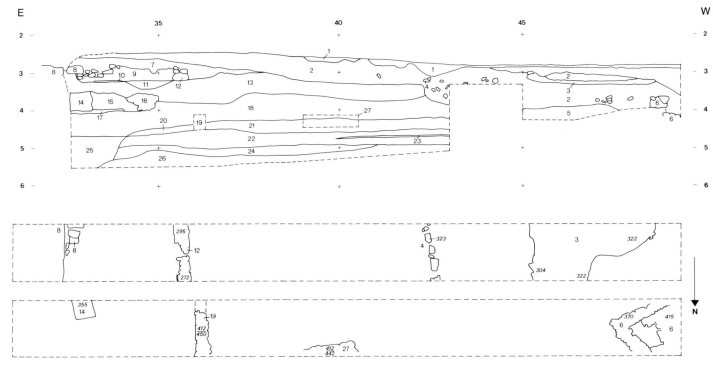

Section 29

Plan descriptions

Plan 1. Temple I, central platform, terrace-walls, inner structures, and western foreland. Partially covered by Temple II. Excavation limits and continued courses stippled. 1:100. A-areas excavated to subsoil. Foundation offerings are marked with registration numbers, in parenthesis if position approximate, and symbol. Circle: pottery beaker, triangle: copper object, square: stone object, star: gold object.

1. Southern terrace-wall Ia, foundation.
2. As 1, wall on 1.
3. Opening in 2.
4. Western terrace wall Ia, north part.
5. As 4, south part, foundation.
6. Western terrace wall IA, wall on 5.
7. Opening between 4 and 5.
8. Northern terrace wall Ia, west part, secondary obverse.
9. Northern terrace wall Ia, west part.
10. Northern terrace wall Ia, east part.
11. Northern terrace wall Ia or chamber walls on 10, cf. plan 2.
12. Southern and eastern terrace wall Ib.
13. Stone-bedding at the bottom of platform.
14. Partition wall in room in the platform's southwestern corner.
15. Opening in 14.
16. Western antechamber and eastern rear chamber in platform, southwestern part.
17. Sunken foundation in 16.
18. As 17.
19. As 17.
20. North wall in 16, antechamber.
21. North wall in 16, rear chamber.
22. East wall in 16, rear chamber.
23. As 22.
24. Stone container (517.ARJ) in clay core, finding-place.
25. Stairway Ia.
26. Stairway Ib.
27. Pool ramp Ia, string blocks.
28. Stones.
29. Foundation stone for 27.
30. As 28.
31. Terrace wall for oval platform.
32. As 31.
33. Stone-setting.
34. Pit.
35. Drainage channel.
36. Drain.
37. Wall fragment.
38. Base stone, western foreland.
39. As 31.

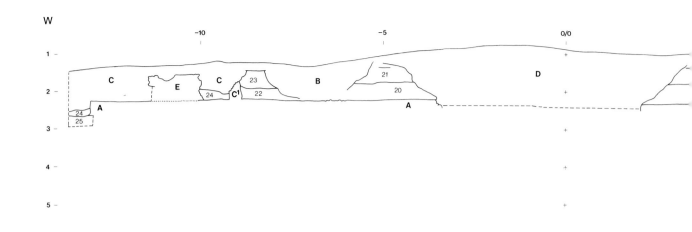

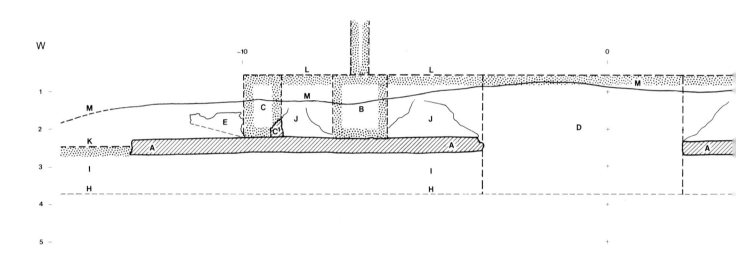

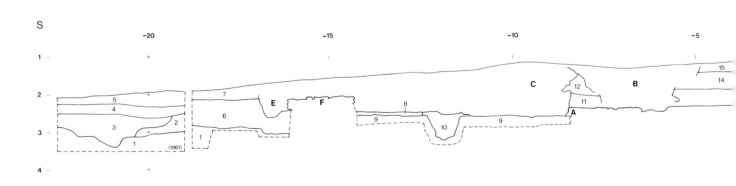

Plan 8. Temple III, the platform's terrace walls, temple well and Islamic masonry. Course continuation broken. 1:100.

1. Western terrace wall, dragged-out block south of this, broken.
2. Northern terrace wall.
3. Base stone with depressions.
4. As 3.
5. Eastern terrace wall.
6. Local masonry.
7. Southwest corner of terrace wall.
8. Remains of second well drum from below, Temple III.
9. Bottom well drum, Temple III.
10. Well shaft, Temple IIb.
11. Well shaft, Temple IIa.
12. Islamic masonry.
13. As 12.
14. As 12 (?).

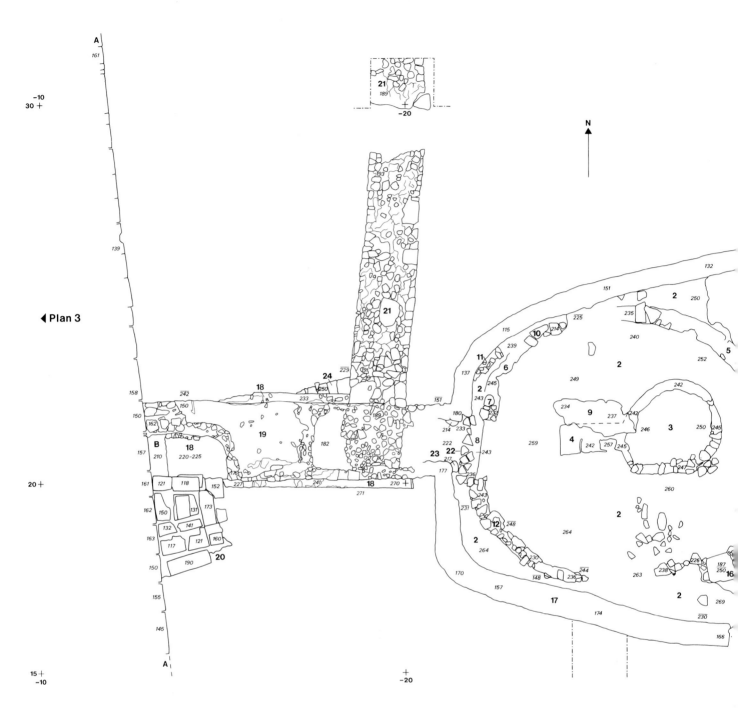

◀ Plan 3

Contributors

H.Hellmuth Andersen
Moesgård Museum
8270 Højbjerg
Denmark

Søren F. Andersen
Department of Classical Archaeology
University of Aarhus
8000 Århus
Denmark

Pernille Bangsgaard
The Carsten Niebuhr Institute
University of Copenhagen
2300 København S
Denmark

Michèle Casanova
Département Histoire de l'Art et Archéologie
Université de Rennes 2, Haute Bretagne
Campus Villejean, Place du recteur Le Moal
CS 24307,
35043 Rennes Cedex,
France

Dennis L. Heskel
formerly
Department of Anthropology
University of Utah
Salt Lake City

United States
Flemming Højlund
Moesgård Museum
8270 Højbjerg
Denmark

Derek Kennet
Department of Archaeology
University of Durham
Durham
England

Poul Kjærum
Moesgård Museum
8270 Højbjerg
Denmark

† Edward Sangmeister
Arbeitsgemeinschaft für Metallurgie des Alter-
tums bei dem Römisch-Germanischen Zentralmu-
seum Institut für Ur- und Frühgeschicte
Freiburg
Germany

Margareta Tengberg
UMR 7041
Maison de l'Archéologie et de l'Ethnologie
Nanterre
France

Plan 2. Temple I, central platform, floor horizon. Partially covered by Temple II. 1:100.

1. Plaster floor, with pits in the south-west.
2. Rubble layers or broken-up parts in 1.
3. Archaeological breaches in 1.
4. Semicircular elevation of 1.
5. Drain under 1.
6. As 5.
7. As 5.
8. As 5.
9. Wall around "cella".
10. Wall around chamber.
11. As 10.
12. Small wall in the corner of walls 10 and 11.
13-18. As 10.
19. Plaster foundation.
20. Dressed limestone block.
21. As 20.
22. Step-shaped platform.
23. Altar structure.
24. Round structure.
25. As 24.
26. Circular altar block, deposition from Temple II (?).

▲ALO

30 +

III

●▲
(AMB)

166
153

163

138

343   142

154
163

326   257

II   II

36

257

290

A

272

II

35

280
263

268

4

24
ARJ ■ ■ ARK

311

338

352

341

34

268

271

268

33

(AMA)

38

37

356

638

II

II

271

(ALI) ■ ■
▲ (ALJ)
☆ (ALK)

II

29   284

20 183
332

171
272

II

237

17

7

298

27   297 299 298

298

302

305   II

296

221 197

29

286

(AOP)

5

192
246

18

256

322

300

337 319

357

261
343

238

265
350

16   A

378

347

5

5

25

333
345

210
293

19

6

26   240

273

289

300
321

265

278

3

2

6

II

342

295
348

6

368 342

12

28

10 +
25

20 +
20

10 +
10

30

II

32

II

III

31

504
536

526
542

Plan 4. Temple II, central platform, western part. Walls are hatched. Shallow dressing on the surface of ashlars is indicated by pricking. 1:100.

A. Plaster floor, Temple I.
B. Western terrace wall.
C. Pool stairway.
D. As B, but robbed.
E. Stone-robbers' breach in A.
F-H. As E.
J. Foundation wall for L's continuation, cf. plan 3.
K. Foundation wall for L.
L. Course of wall on J.

M. Floor flags.
N. Impression of M.
O. Wall ledge.
P. As O.
Q. Course of wall.
R. As Q.
S. Plaster floor.
T. Layer of plaster.
U. As S.
V. Disturbance.
X. "Stair".
Y. Plaster stud.
Z. Course of wall.

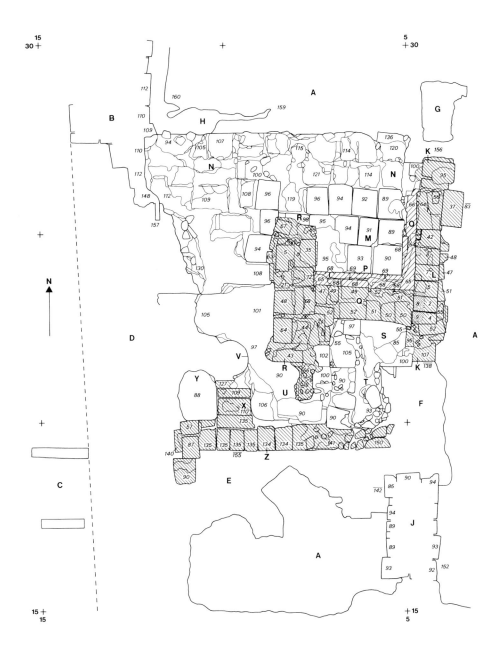

Plan 4

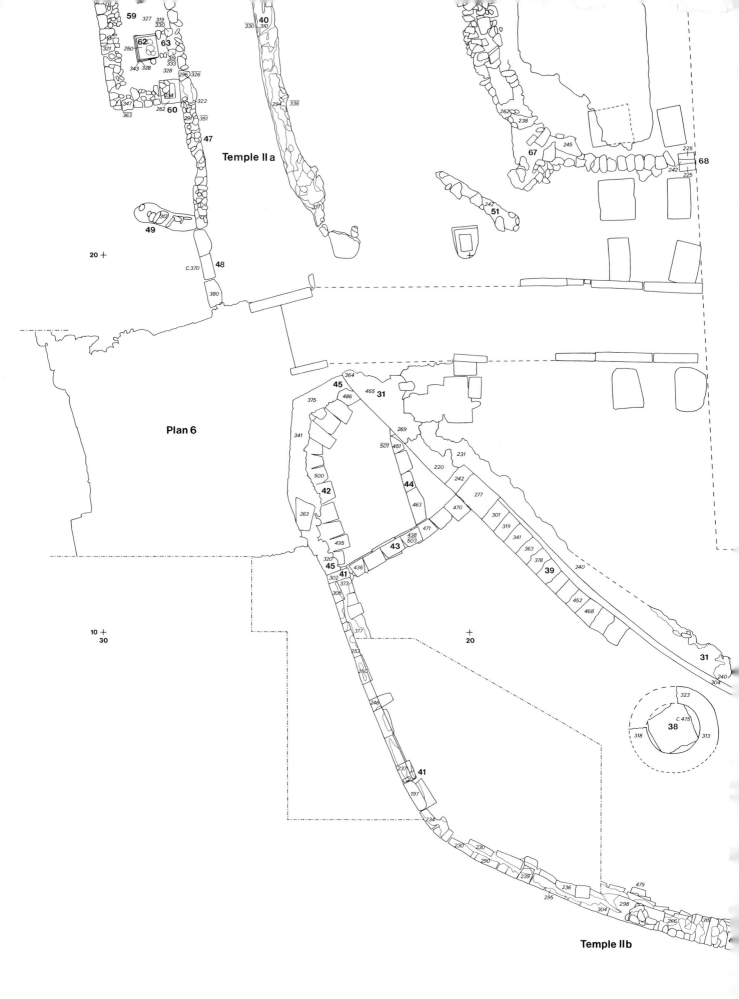

Temple II a

59

62 63

47

49

48

20 +

C.370

380

Plan 6

10 +
30

40

67

51

68

45   31

45

42

44

43

41

39

31

38

41

Temple IIb

Plan 6. Temple II, pool and staircase. Excavation limits dot-and-dashed and continued courses broken, cf. section 33. 1:100.

1. West room in pool.
2. East room in pool.
3. West wall in 1.
4. Channel opening.
5. South wall in 1.
6. Channel opening.
7. As 6.
8. North wall in 1.
9. Channel opening.
10. East wall in 1.
11. Block in 10.
12. As 11.
13. Basin in 1.
14. Block in 1.
15. Stone vessel on blocks in 1.
16. Block in 1.
17. As 16.
18-20. Floor flags in 2.
21. North wall in 2.
22-26. South wall in 2, terraced.
27. East wall in 2, upper part.

28. Foundation for 27.
29. East wall in 2, lower part.
30. Oval wall IIb, wall kink.
31. Older wall analogous to 27 and 29.
32. Older east chamber in pool (?).
33. Wall superimposed on 5.
34-41. Lower steps in pool stair.
42. Portal step.
43. Cast plaster hole.
44. Foundation for stair wall.
45. Stair strings.
46. Foundation for 45.
47-54. Flanking plinth-stones.
55. Portal foundation.
56. As 55.
57. Wall fragment west of 56.
58. Channel south of pool, from 7.
59. Chamber south of pool, built onto oval wall IIb.
60. Masonry west of pool.
61-62. As 60.

A. Central platform, western terrace-wall, robbed.
B. Oval wall IIa.
C. Oval wall IIb.

Plan 5. Temple II, northern oval platform, two separate plans. Excavation boundaries dot-and-dashed. 1:100.

1. Northwestern part of oval wall IIb, direct continuation of plan 3 (46).
2. As 1 in the north.
3. Stone altar.
4. Circular block.

20
+

N

50 +

$\frac{300}{310}$

+

1

$\frac{300}{320}$

40 +

+

$\frac{305}{325}$

Plan 3
▼

Plan 3. Temple II, central platform (1-30), oval platform (31-68), cf. supplementary plan 4 with west part of central platform, plan 5 with oval platform to the north, plan 6 with pool and plan 7 with the Eastern Court. Wall of building on Temple II platform hatched. Shallow dressing on the surface of ashlars is indicated by pricking. Excavation limits dot-and-dashed and continued courses broken. 1:100.

1. Eastern terrace wall.
2. Drain channel in 1.
3. Drain for 2, crossing 1.
4. Southern terrace wall, robbed.
5. Western terrace wall.
6. Northern terrace-wall.
7. Foundation wall.
8. Course of wall on 7.
9. Course of wall on 1.
10. Course of wall.
11. As 7.
12. Floor.
13. Estrade on 12.
14. Plaster elevation on 12.
15. Channel to 3 and 2.
16. Framing.
17. Circular stone-setting under floor level.
18. Circular altars, circle stones A-P, rim-stones Q-AC, and circular altar block, AD, under floor level.
19. Gable stone *in situ*.
20. As 19, tumbled.
21. Stand impression for 20.
22. Stone with depression.
23. Stone with channel.
24. "Yoni".
25. Pierced stone, tumbled.
26. "Step".
27. As 25, *in situ*.
28-29. As 27.
30. As 27, but *ex situ*.

31. Oval wall IIa, in the south and south-west.
32. Cross-wall on 31.
33. Stair frontally on 31.
34. As 32.
35. Course of wall.
36. Stone circle at foot of 31.
37. As 36.
38. Temple well, square shaft in phase IIa, round in phase IIb.
39. Stair on the side of 31 to 38.
40. Oval wall IIa in the west.
41. Oval wall IIb in the south and south-west.
42. As 41, special continuation.
43. Cross-wall on 41.
44. Cross-wall on 43.
45. Secondary continuation of 41.
46. Oval wall IIb in the west.
47. As 46.
48. Course of wall in continuation of 47.
49. Cross-wall on 47.
50. Altar structure above 33.
51. Wall fragment.
52. Oval structure.
53. Inner structure in 52.
54. Plaster floor in 53.
55. Foundation for 54.
56. Stair.
57. Cross-wall.
58. As 57.
59. Rectangular platform.
60. Block on 59.
61-62. As 60.
63. Small walls on 59.
64. Plinth-stone, fragment.
65. Block.
66. As 64.
67. Drain.
68. Gutter-stone for 67.

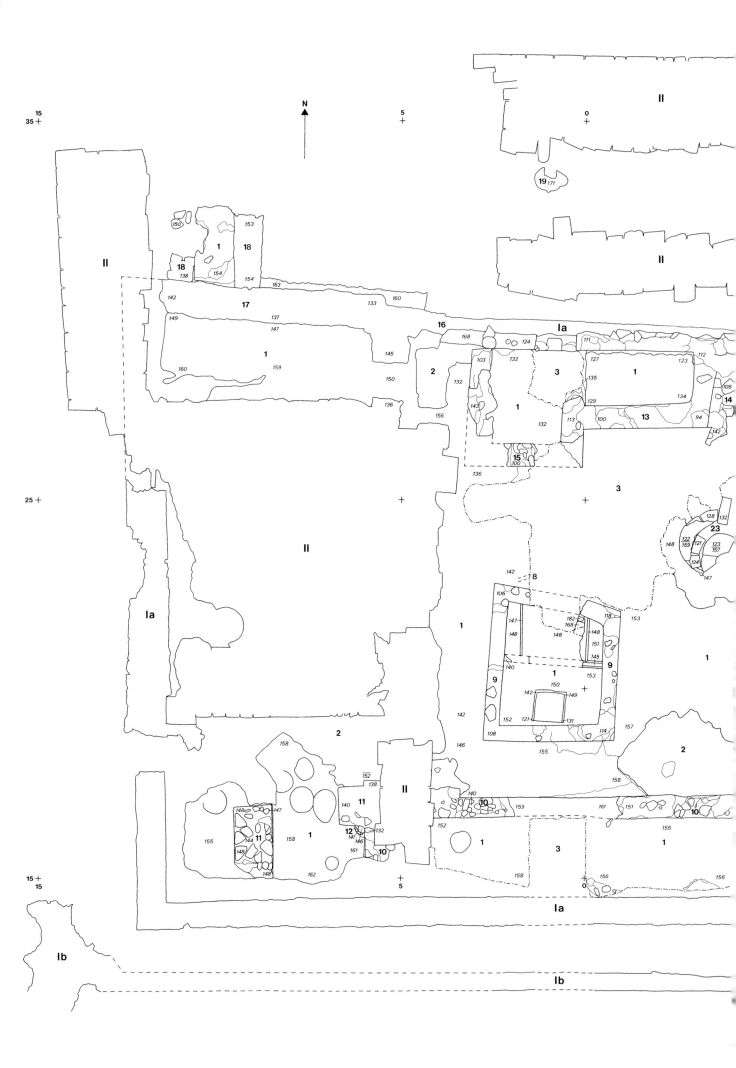

Plan 7. Temple II, the Eastern Court with ramp, ramp road and conduits. Excavation limits dot-and-dashed and continued courses broken. 1:100.

1. Oldest exposed building parts.
2. Plaster floor.
3. Ring-shaped structure on 2.
4. Rectangular platform on 2.
5. Masonry on 2.
6. Impression as 5.
7. As 5.
8. Plaster step.
9. Plaster floor over 2 and 4.
10. Masonry over 2.
11-13. As 10.
14. Plastered channel.
15. Plastered pit.
16. Plaster block.
17. Oval wall.
18. Lower ramp.
19. Upper ramp.
20. Remains of steps on 19 and A.
21. Ramp way.
22. Part of ramp deprived of flags.
23. As 22.
24. Drain.
25. Channel.

A. Temple II, eastern terrace wall.
B. Temple Ib, eastern terrace wall.

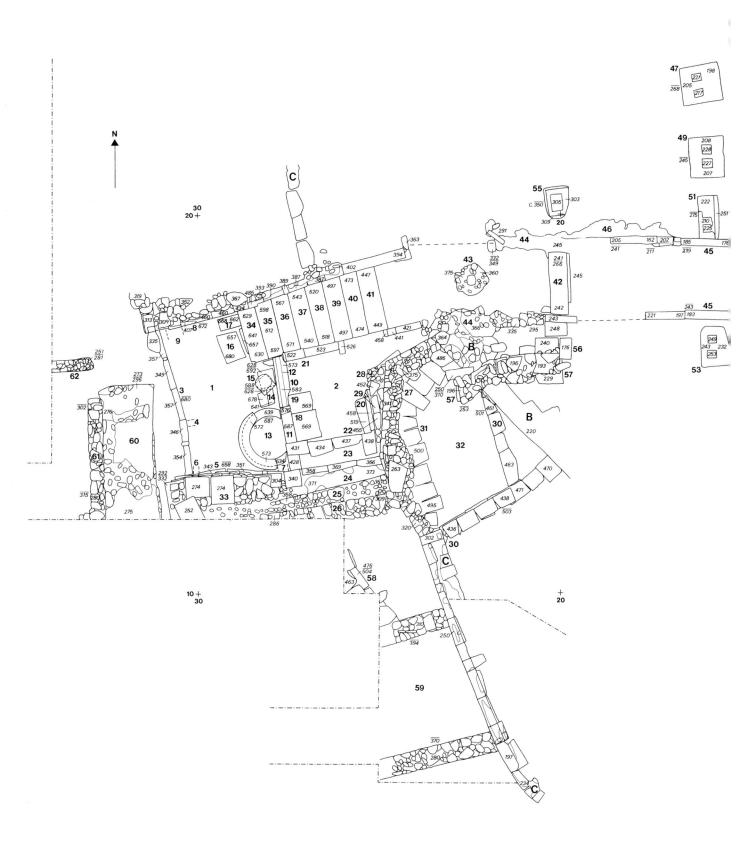

Jutland Archaeological Society Publications on Near Eastern Archaeology

All prices are exclusive of VAT and postage. Members of *The Jutland Archaeological Society* and *The Royal Society for Northern Antiquaries* get a discount of 30% on all orders sent directly to Jutland Archaeological Society, Moesgård Museum, DK-8270 Højbjerg.